Better Homes and Gardens®

Eat Healthy Lose Weight

Volume 7

Meredith Consumer Marketing
Des Moines, Iowa

Better Homes and Gardens.

Eat Healthy Lose Weight

MEREDITH CONSUMER MARKETING
Vice President, Consumer Marketing: Janet Donnelly
Consumer Marketing Product Director: Heather Sorensen
Consumer Marketing Product Manager: Wendy Merical
Business Director: Ron Clingman
Senior Production Manager: Al Rodruck

WATERBURY PUBLICATIONS, INC.
Editorial Director: Lisa Kingsley
Associate Editors: Tricia Bergman, Mary Williams
Creative Director: Ken Carlson
Associate Design Director: Doug Samuelson
Production Assistant: Mindy Samuelson
Contributing Copy Editors: Gretchen Kauffman, Peg Smith
Contributing Indexer: Elizabeth T. Parson

BETTER HOMES AND GARDENS MAGAZINE
Editor in Chief: Gayle Goodson Butler
Senior Deputy Editor, Food & Entertaining: Nancy Wall Hopkins

MEREDITH NATIONAL MEDIA GROUP
President: Tom Harty

MEREDITH CORPORATION
Chairman and Chief Executive Officer: Stephen M. Lacy

In Memoriam: E.T. Meredith III (1933–2003)

Test Kitchen

Our seal assures you that every recipe in *Eat Healthy, Lose Weight* Vol. 7 has been tested in the Better Homes and Gardens® Test Kitchen. This means that each recipe is practical and reliable and meets our high standards of taste appeal. We guarantee your satisfaction with this book for as long as you own it.

All of us at Meredith Consumer Marketing are dedicated to providing you with information and ideas to enhance your home. We welcome your comments and suggestions. Write to us at: Meredith Consumer Marketing, 1716 Locust St., Des Moines, IA 50309-3023.

Pictured on front cover:
Banana Pancakes with Chocolate Bits and Raspberries, page 24

Contents

EAT BETTER NOW

It's been well-established that fad diets don't work long-term. The tried-and-true strategy for losing weight is to change the way that you eat for life. And all of the foods that you need in order to eat healthfully, stave off cravings, and drop excess pounds are in supermarkets—and in this book. Wholesome ingredients plus healthful cooking methods equal the ideal weight-loss equation. The recipes in *Eat Healthy, Lose Weight* Vol. 7 rely on lean proteins, whole grains, and fresh fruits and vegetables for delicious meals your family will love.

The guide for compiling the more than 200 recipes in this book is simple: Use ordinary ingredients to create extraordinary recipes that are low in fat, calories, and sodium. The recipes were created for people living in the real world—and each recipe was tested by the Better Homes and Gardens® Test Kitchen, so you can be assured that every one is simple to follow and tastes great. When food doesn't taste good, you don't want to eat it—no matter how good it is for you. If you want to lose weight, stick to a plan that inspires you to meet your goals with satisfying and delicious foods.

The recipes in *Eat Healthy, Lose Weight* are suited for everyday family meals as well as special occasions—from company-special appetizers to hearty casseroles to desserts that taste indulgent while staying well within calorie and fat guidelines. You'll find such recipes as Strawberry and Cream Cheese Waffle Sandwiches, Sirloin Steak with Deep Red Wine Reduction, Tomato-Bacon Breadsticks, Thai Green Chicken Curry, and Raspberry Strudel Croissants, all of which have been specially developed to fit a healthy-eating plan—a plan that will help you live more healthfully with all the flavors you crave.

Change your diet and change your life!

CHAPTER 1

Snacks

Blue Cheese-Apricot Bites

START TO FINISH: 25 minutes

NUTRITION FACTS PER APPETIZER

Calories 30
Fat 2 g
Cholesterol 3 mg
Sodium 31 mg
Carbohydrates 3 g
Fiber 0 g
Protein 1 g

1 teaspoon canola oil
2 tablespoons finely chopped walnuts
2 teaspoons sugar
½ teaspoon snipped fresh rosemary or ¼ teaspoon dried rosemary, finely crushed
¼ cup crumbled blue cheese (1 ounce)
1 ounce reduced-fat cream cheese (Neufchâtel)
16 dried apricots
Fresh rosemary (optional)

1. In a small skillet heat oil over medium heat. Add walnuts and sugar; cook and stir for 2 to 3 minutes or until walnuts are lightly toasted. Stir in ½ teaspoon fresh or ¼ teaspoon dried rosemary; cook and stir for 30 seconds more. Transfer nuts to a foil-lined baking sheet; cool.

2. Meanwhile, in a small mixing bowl combine blue cheese and cream cheese. Beat with an electric mixer on medium speed until smooth.

3. Spoon about ¾ teaspoon of the cheese mixture on each dried apricot. Sprinkle with nuts. If desired, garnish with additional fresh rosemary. **MAKES 16 APPETIZERS**

Two-Tomato Bruschetta

PREP: 10 minutes
BAKE: 5 minutes
OVEN: 350°F

NUTRITION FACTS
PER 2 BRUSCHETTA

Calories 181
Fat 11 g
Cholesterol 8 mg
Sodium 344 mg
Carbohydrates 18 g
Fiber 2 g
Protein 6 g

⅓ cup crumbled feta cheese with tomato and basil
⅓ cup dried tomatoes (not oil-packed), chopped
2 tablespoons snipped fresh basil
2 tablespoons snipped fresh Italian (flat-leaf) parsley
2 tablespoons olive oil
¼ teaspoon freshly ground black pepper
1 clove garlic, minced
8 to 10 slices whole grain baguette (each slice ½ inch thick)
2 roma tomatoes, thinly sliced

1. Preheat oven to 350°F. In a small bowl combine feta cheese, dried tomatoes, basil, and parsley. Set aside.

2. In another small bowl stir together oil, pepper, and garlic. Evenly brush oil mixture on bread slices. Place bread on a large baking sheet.

3. Bake about 5 minutes or until lightly toasted. Remove from oven. Top with tomato slices. Spoon feta cheese mixture on tomato slices. Serve immediately or broil 3 to 4 inches from the heat for 1 to 2 minutes or until cheese is slightly melted. **MAKES 4 SERVINGS**

Tomato-Bacon Breadsticks

PREP: 20 minutes
STAND: 5 minutes
BAKE: 8 minutes
OVEN: 425°F

NUTRITION FACTS PER BREADSTICK

Calories 94   *Fat* 5 g   *Cholesterol* 6 mg   *Sodium* 251 mg   *Carbohydrates* 9 g   *Fiber* 1 g   *Protein* 3 g

4   slices turkey bacon
¼   cup dried tomatoes (not oil-packed)
     Boiling water
1   cup all-purpose flour
½   cup whole wheat pastry flour or whole wheat flour
2   teaspoons baking powder
½   teaspoon salt
¼   teaspoon cream of tartar
2   tablespoons chopped green onion tops
⅓   cup 60 to 70 percent vegetable oil spread, chilled
1   tablespoon butter
½   cup fat-free milk
     Nonstick cooking spray
¼   cup grated Parmesan cheese (1 ounce)

1. Preheat oven to 425°F. Cook bacon according to package directions; cool slightly, then crumble or chop bacon. Set aside. Place tomatoes in a small bowl. Add enough boiling water to cover; let stand for 5 minutes. Drain tomatoes, discarding the liquid. Finely chop tomatoes. Set aside.

2. In a medium bowl stir together all-purpose flour, whole wheat flour, baking powder, salt, and cream of tartar. Stir in green onion tops. Using a pastry blender, cut in vegetable oil spread and butter until mixture resembles coarse crumbs. Stir in crumbled bacon and chopped tomatoes. Make a well in the center of the flour mixture. Add milk all at once; stir just until dough clings together.

3. Turn out dough onto a lightly floured surface. Knead by folding and gently pressing dough for four to six strokes or until nearly smooth. Roll dough into an 8-inch square. Cut into 1-inch-wide strips; cut each strip in half crosswise. If desired, twist each strip.

4. Place strips 1 inch apart on an ungreased baking sheet. Coat with cooking spray; sprinkle with Parmesan cheese. Bake for 8 to 10 minutes or until tops are golden brown. Serve warm.
MAKES 16 BREADSTICKS

Fruit Chutney with Spiced Chips

PREP: 25 minutes
SLOW COOK: 2 hours (high)

NUTRITION FACTS PER SERVING

Calories 114
Fat 2 g
Cholesterol 4 mg
Sodium 182 mg
Carbohydrates 21 g
Fiber 2 g
Protein 3 g

2 large apples, such as Braeburn, cored and cut into 1-inch pieces
2 large pears, such as Anjou, cored and cut into 1-inch pieces
1 sweet onion, chopped
1 cup fresh or frozen whole cranberries, thawed
⅓ cup packed brown sugar
¼ cup balsamic vinegar
1 teaspoon ground cinnamon
1 teaspoon ground ginger
⅛ teaspoon salt
1 tablespoon cornstarch
2 tablespoons cold water
1 recipe Spiced Chips
4 ounces goat cheese (chèvre), crumbled

1. For fruit chutney, in a 3½- or 4-quart slow cooker combine apples, pears, onion, cranberries, brown sugar, vinegar, cinnamon, ginger, and salt.

2. Cover and cook on high-heat setting for 1 hour. In a small bowl combine cornstarch and the cold water; stir into cooker. Cover and cook on high-heat setting for 1 hour more.

3. Serve chutney warm or at room temperature with Spiced Chips. Top each serving with crumbled goat cheese. **MAKES 24 SERVINGS**

Spiced Chips: Preheat oven to 400°F. Cut 9 whole wheat tortillas in half, then cut each half in wide strips (8 strips per tortilla). Place tortilla strips in a single layer on baking sheets. Lightly coat wedges with nonstick cooking spray. In a small bowl mix together ½ teaspoon granulated sugar and ¼ teaspoon ground coriander. Sprinkle over tortilla strips. Bake for 10 minutes, turning once halfway through baking. Makes 72 chips.

Baked Root Vegetable Chips

PREP: 10 minutes
BAKE: 14 minutes
STAND: 5 minutes
OVEN: 375°F

NUTRITION FACTS PER SERVING

Calories 56
Fat 0 g
Cholesterol 0 mg
Sodium 181 mg
Carbohydrates 13 g
Fiber 2 g
Protein 1 g

	Nonstick cooking spray
2	sweet potatoes, purple beets, or golden beets,* peeled
¼	teaspoon salt
¼	teaspoon ground black pepper

1. Preheat oven to 375°F. Lightly coat two large baking sheets with cooking spray.

2. Use a mandoline to slice vegetables ¹⁄₁₆ inch thick. For beets, sandwich slices between layers of paper towels and press firmly to remove excess liquid. Arrange vegetable slices in a single layer on the prepared baking sheets. Coat the tops of the vegetable slices with cooking spray; sprinkle with salt and pepper.

3. Bake for 10 minutes. Remove baking sheets from oven; let stand for 5 minutes. Return baking sheets to oven. Bake for 4 to 8 minutes more, removing baking sheets to check for doneness every minute after 4 minutes. Chips are done when the center of each chip no longer looks wet. Transfer chips to paper towels. Cool for 5 minutes to crisp the chips. **MAKES 4 SERVINGS**

*Tip: Try a combination of these vegetables. To avoid burning, check for doneness frequently and remove each type of chip as it is done.

Make-Ahead Directions: Store cooled chips in an airtight container up to 24 hours. If necessary, re-crisp chips in a 325°F oven for 3 to 4 minutes.

Spicy-Savory Snack Mix

PREP: 10 minutes
BAKE: 8 minutes
OVEN: 375°F

NUTRITION FACTS PER ¼-CUP SERVING

Calories 162   *Fat* 11 g   *Cholesterol* 4 mg   *Sodium* 146 mg   *Carbohydrates* 14 g   *Fiber* 2 g   *Protein* 4 g

1   cup whole almonds or peanuts
¾   cup pecan halves
¼   cup hazelnuts (filberts)
2   tablespoons butter
2   tablespoons finely snipped
    fresh rosemary or 1 teaspoon
    dried rosemary, crushed
2   tablespoons packed brown
    sugar
2   teaspoons soy sauce
½   to 1 teaspoon crushed
    red pepper
3   cups pretzel nuggets

1. Preheat oven to 375°F. In a 15×10×1-inch baking pan evenly spread almonds, pecans, and hazelnuts. Bake about 8 minutes or until nuts are lightly toasted, stirring once or twice.

2. Meanwhile, in a large saucepan melt butter over medium heat. Remove from heat. Stir in rosemary, brown sugar, soy sauce, and crushed red pepper. Add nuts and pretzels to butter mixture; toss gently to coat. Spread nut mix in the baking pan; let cool.
MAKES 16 SERVINGS (4 CUPS)

Make-Ahead Directions:
Prepare mix as directed. Place in an airtight container. Cover and store in the refrigerator up to 1 month or in the freezer up to 3 months.

Rosemary Roasted Nuts

PREP: 15 minutes
BAKE: 12 minutes
OVEN: 375°F

NUTRITION FACTS PER 3-TABLESPOON SERVING

Calories 177
Fat 15 g
Cholesterol 2 mg
Sodium 60 mg
Carbohydrates 5 g
Fiber 2 g
Protein 6 g

3   cups whole unblanched almonds
1½ cups walnuts
1   cup raw pumpkin seeds (pepitas)
2   tablespoons finely snipped fresh rosemary
2   teaspoons packed brown sugar
1   teaspoon sea salt
½   teaspoon cayenne pepper
2   tablespoons butter, melted

1. Preheat oven to 375°F. In a 15×10×1-inch baking pan combine almonds, walnuts, and pumpkin seeds. Bake about 12 minutes or until toasted, stirring once.

2. In a small bowl combine rosemary, brown sugar, salt, and cayenne pepper. Stir in butter. Drizzle butter mixture over nuts, tossing gently to coat. Serve warm, or cool to room temperature.

MAKES 30 SERVINGS (ABOUT 5½ CUPS)

Make-Ahead Directions: Cool nuts to room temperature. Place cooled nuts in an airtight container. Store at room temperature up to 3 days.

Apples with Maple-Cinnamon Dip

START TO FINISH: 10 minutes

NUTRITION FACTS
PER 3 TABLESPOONS DIP
+ ½ CUP APPLE SLICES

Calories 146
Fat 7 g
Cholesterol 21 mg
Sodium 97 mg
Carbohydrates 21 g
Fiber 2 g
Protein 3 g

4 ounces reduced-fat cream
  cheese (Neufchâtel)
2 tablespoons pure maple syrup
¾ teaspoon ground cinnamon
¼ cup chopped walnuts or
  pecans, toasted* (optional)
2 cups thinly sliced apples
  (2 medium)

1. For dip, in a food processor
combine cream cheese, maple
syrup, and cinnamon. Cover and
process until smooth. Transfer
dip to a serving bowl. If desired,
sprinkle with toasted walnuts.
Serve with apple slices.
MAKES 4 SERVINGS

*Tip: To toast nuts, spread them
in a shallow baking pan. Bake in
a 350°F oven for 5 to 10 minutes
or until light brown, shaking pan
once or twice. Watch carefully to
prevent nuts from burning.

Edamame Hummus

START TO FINISH: 20 minutes

NUTRITION FACTS PER 2 TABLESPOONS

Calories 81   *Fat* 6 g   *Cholesterol* 0 mg   *Sodium* 78 mg   *Carbohydrates* 5 g   *Fiber* 1 g   *Protein* 3 g

1   10-ounce package frozen sweet soybeans (edamame)
½   cup snipped fresh Italian (flat-leaf) parsley
¼   cup lemon juice
¼   cup water
1   tablespoon tahini (sesame seed paste)
½   teaspoon salt
½   teaspoon ground cumin
3   cloves garlic, peeled and quartered
⅓   cup olive oil
⅛   teaspoon paprika (optional)
8   cups assorted vegetables, such as sweet pepper pieces, cucumber slices, baby carrots, snow pea pods, and/or celery sticks

1. Cook edamame until tender according to package directions; drain.

2. In a food processor combine edamame, parsley, lemon juice, the water, tahini, salt, cumin, and garlic. Cover and process until smooth. With food processor running, slowly add oil in a thin steady stream, processing until smooth. Add additional water if necessary to reach desired consistency. If desired, sprinkle with paprika. Serve with vegetables for dipping/scooping.
MAKES 16 SERVINGS (2 CUPS)

Lima Bean Hummus with Toasted Pita Crisps

PREP: 25 minutes
COOK: 10 minutes
BAKE: 5 minutes
OVEN: 400°F

NUTRITION FACTS PER SERVING

Calories 129
Fat 1 g
Cholesterol 1 mg
Sodium 237 mg
Carbohydrates 25 g
Fiber 4 g
Protein 6 g

1 10-ounce package frozen lima beans
1 6-ounce carton plain low-fat yogurt
2 shallots, peeled and coarsely chopped
2 tablespoons lemon juice
1 tablespoon honey
1 tablespoon chopped fresh chives
2 cloves garlic
½ teaspoon ground black pepper
¼ teaspoon salt
3 whole grain pita bread rounds
   Nonstick cooking spray

1. In a medium saucepan cook lima beans in a small amount of boiling water for 10 minutes; drain.

2. In a food processor combine lima beans, yogurt, shallots, lemon juice, honey, chives, garlic, pepper, and salt. Cover and process until smooth.

3. Preheat oven to 400°F. Halve pita bread rounds horizontally. Cut into wedges. Place on a baking sheet. Lightly coat pita wedges with cooking spray. Bake 5 to 8 minutes or until lightly browned and crisp. Serve hummus with pita crisps. **MAKES 8 SERVINGS**

Black Bean Salsa

PREP: 20 minutes
CHILL: 4 hours

NUTRITION FACTS PER SERVING

Calories 47
Fat 2 g
Cholesterol 0 mg
Sodium 136 mg
Carbohydrates 8 g
Fiber 2 g
Protein 3 g

1   15-ounce can black beans, rinsed and drained
1½ cups chopped and seeded cucumber (1 medium)
½   cup chopped tomato (1 medium)
½   cup sliced green onions (4)
¼   cup lime juice
1   tablespoon snipped fresh cilantro
1   tablespoon olive oil
½   teaspoon ground cumin
⅛   teaspoon salt
⅛   teaspoon cayenne pepper
    Baked tortilla chips

1. In a medium bowl combine beans, cucumber, tomato, green onions, lime juice, cilantro, oil, cumin, salt, and cayenne pepper. Cover and chill for 4 to 24 hours. Serve with tortilla chips.
MAKES 10 SERVINGS

Chipotle Kettle Corn

START TO FINISH: 15 minutes

NUTRITION FACTS PER 1 CUP

Calories 78   *Fat* 3 g   *Cholesterol* 0 mg   *Sodium* 266 mg   *Carbohydrates* 15 g   *Fiber* 1 g   *Protein* 1 g

1   cup sugar
2   teaspoons salt
2   teaspoons ground cumin
1   teaspoon ground chipotle
     chile pepper
⅓   cup canola oil
⅔   cup popcorn kernels

1. For chipotle seasoning, in a small bowl combine sugar, salt, cumin, and chipotle pepper; set aside.

2. Heat the oil in an 8-quart pan over medium-high heat. Add the popcorn and cook for 2 minutes, shaking pan occasionally. Add ½ cup of the chipotle seasoning. Cover and cook until popcorn begins to pop, shaking pan often. Once popcorn begins to pop, shake continuously until the popping slows. Immediately remove pan from heat and carefully pour into a large serving bowl (popcorn will be very hot).

3. Place remaining chipotle seasoning in a shaker jar; sprinkle some on the popped corn. Pass remaining seasoning.
MAKES 16 SERVINGS (16 CUPS)

Microwave Directions: Prepare seasoning as directed. One at a time, pop two 3.3-ounce bags of microwave kettle corn. Immediately after popping, pour popcorn into an extra-large bowl and toss with 2 tablespoons of the seasoning. Repeat with remaining bag of popcorn. Pass remaining seasoning. Makes 20 (1-cup) servings.

Ultimate Berry Smoothie

START TO FINISH: 15 minutes

NUTRITION FACTS PER SERVING

Calories 242
Fat 5 g
Cholesterol 0 mg
Sodium 50 mg
Carbohydrates 42 g
Fiber 7 g
Protein 9 g

4　cups fresh or frozen mixed berries
1　12.3-ounce package silken-style tofu (fresh bean curd) (1½ cups)
1　cup unsweetened cranberry-raspberry juice
¼　cup flaxseed meal
3　tablespoons honey
　　Fresh raspberries and/or blueberries (optional)

1. In a blender combine the mixed berries, tofu, cranberry-raspberry juice, flaxseed meal, and honey. Cover and blend until smooth. If desired, garnish with fresh raspberries and/or blueberries.
MAKES 4 (12-OUNCE) SERVINGS

CHAPTER 2 Breakfast

Banana Pancakes with Chocolate Bits and Raspberries

START TO FINISH: 25 minutes

NUTRITION FACTS PER SERVING

Calories 314
Fat 7 g
Cholesterol 49 mg
Sodium 606 mg
Carbohydrates 60 g
Fiber 8 g
Protein 9 g

1¼ cups whole wheat flour
2   teaspoons baking powder
½   teaspoon salt
1   egg, lightly beaten
⅔   cup low-fat milk
½   cup mashed ripe banana
½   cup light maple-flavor syrup
2   ounces semisweet chocolate, finely chopped
    Nonstick cooking spray
    Light butter (optional)
1   cup fresh raspberries

1. In a medium bowl stir together whole wheat flour, baking powder, and salt. In a small bowl combine egg, milk, mashed banana, and 1 tablespoon of the syrup. Add egg mixture all at once to flour mixture. Stir just until moistened (batter should be slightly lumpy). Fold in chocolate.

2. Coat a nonstick griddle or heavy skillet with cooking spray; heat griddle over medium-low heat. For each pancake, pour ¼ cup of the batter onto hot griddle; spread if necessary. Cook about 2 minutes. Turn pancakes when surfaces are bubbly, edges are slightly dry, and bottom is golden. Cook about 2 minutes more.

3. In a small saucepan heat the remaining syrup until warm. Serve warm pancakes with syrup and, if desired, butter. Top with raspberries. **MAKES 4 SERVINGS**

Buttermilk Bran Cakes with Apple-Walnut Topping

START TO FINISH: 30 minutes

NUTRITION FACTS PER SERVING

Calories 319
Fat 10 g
Cholesterol 57 mg
Sodium 559 mg
Carbohydrates 52 g
Fiber 5 g
Protein 10 g

⅓ cup high-fiber wheat bran cereal
1¼ cups buttermilk or sour milk*
1 egg, lightly beaten
2 tablespoons packed brown sugar
2 teaspoons canola oil
1 cup all-purpose flour
1 teaspoon baking powder
½ teaspoon baking soda
¼ teaspoon salt
1 cup chopped apple
¼ cup coarsely chopped walnuts
1 tablespoon granulated sugar
¼ teaspoon ground cinnamon
⅓ cup vanilla low-fat yogurt
  Nonstick cooking spray
  Ground cinnamon (optional)

1. Place cereal in a medium bowl. Add buttermilk, egg, brown sugar, and oil; stir to mix well. Let stand for 10 minutes. Meanwhile, in a small bowl stir together flour, baking powder, baking soda, and salt; set aside.

2. For apple-walnut topping, in a small bowl combine apple and walnuts. Combine granulated sugar and the ¼ teaspoon cinnamon; toss with apple mixture. Stir yogurt until creamy; gently stir into apple mixture.

3. Add flour mixture to buttermilk mixture, stirring until combined. Coat a nonstick griddle or heavy skillet with cooking spray; heat griddle over medium-low heat. For each pancake, pour ¼ cup of the batter onto hot griddle. Cook for 1 to 2 minutes or until bottom is golden. Turn pancake; cook about 1 minute more or until golden. Transfer to a serving platter; keep warm while cooking the remaining pancakes. Serve pancakes with apple-walnut topping. If desired, sprinkle with additional cinnamon.
MAKES 4 SERVINGS

*Tip: To make 1¼ cups sour milk, place 4 teaspoons lemon juice or vinegar in a glass measuring cup. Add enough milk to equal 1¼ cups total liquid; stir. Let stand for 5 minutes before using.

Cornmeal Waffles with Blueberry Compote

START TO FINISH: 25 minutes

NUTRITION FACTS PER SERVING

Calories 204   *Fat* 7 g   *Cholesterol* 54 mg   *Sodium* 176 mg   *Carbohydrates* 31 g   *Fiber* 2 g   *Protein* 5 g

¾   cup all-purpose flour
½   cup yellow or white cornmeal
2   tablespoons packed brown sugar
1   teaspoon baking powder
¼   teaspoon salt
1   cup buttermilk or sour milk*
½   cup fat-free milk
2   egg yolks
3   tablespoons canola oil
½   teaspoon vanilla
2   egg whites
1   recipe Blueberry Compote
    Nonstick cooking spray
    Fresh blueberries, raspberries, and/or strawberries (optional)

1. In a large bowl combine flour, cornmeal, brown sugar, baking powder, and salt.

2. In a medium bowl combine buttermilk, milk, egg yolks, oil, and vanilla. Whisk to combine. Whisk buttermilk mixture into flour mixture just until combined (do not overmix).

3. In a large mixing bowl beat egg whites with an electric mixer on medium-high speed until soft peaks form. Gently fold egg whites into batter.

4. Coat a waffle iron with cooking spray; heat according to the manufacturer's directions. For each waffle, pour about ¾ cup batter into grids.** Close lid quickly; do not open until done. Bake according to manufacturer's directions. Serve warm with Blueberry Compote and, if desired, fresh berries. **MAKES 8 SERVINGS**

Blueberry Compote: In a medium saucepan bring 1 cup apple juice and 1 tablespoon lemon juice to boiling; reduce heat. Simmer, uncovered, for 8 to 10 minutes or until reduced by half. Stir in 2 cups fresh blueberries, ½ teaspoon finely shredded lemon peel, and ⅛ teaspoon ground cinnamon. Return to boiling; reduce heat. Simmer, uncovered, for 5 minutes. Makes 1⅔ cups.

*Tip: To make 1 cup sour milk, place 1 tablespoon lemon juice or vinegar in a glass measuring cup. Add enough milk to equal 1 cup total liquid; stir. Let stand for 5 minutes before using.

**Tip: If using a 6-inch round waffle iron, use ½ cup batter per waffle and serve three quarters of a round waffle per serving.

Strawberry and Cream Cheese Waffle Sandwiches

START TO FINISH: 20 minutes

NUTRITION FACTS PER SANDWICH

Calories 274
Fat 8 g
Cholesterol 13 mg
Sodium 346 mg
Carbohydrates 40 g
Fiber 6 g
Protein 10 g

⅓ cup light cream cheese, softened
4 teaspoons honey
8 slices whole grain sandwich bread
1½ cups sliced fresh strawberries
¼ cup low-fat granola
2 tablespoons salted, roasted sunflower kernels
Nonstick cooking spray
Honey (optional)

1. In a small bowl stir together cream cheese and 4 teaspoons honey. Spread one side of each bread slice with cream cheese mixture. Top four of the bread slices with strawberries, granola, and sunflower kernels. Top with the remaining four bread slices, spread sides down.

2. Coat a waffle iron with cooking spray; heat according to the manufacturer's directions. Cook sandwiches, one at a time, in waffle iron about 2 minutes or until golden. When done, use a fork to lift sandwich off grids. Cut sandwiches into halves or quarters. If desired, serve with additional honey. **MAKES 4 SANDWICHES**

Baked French Toast Strips with Apricot Dipping Sauce

PREP: 15 minutes
BAKE: 12 minutes
OVEN: 450°F

NUTRITION FACTS PER SERVING

Calories 288
Fat 5 g
Cholesterol 62 mg
Sodium 245 mg
Carbohydrates 51 g
Fiber 4 g
Protein 10 g

Nonstick cooking spray
¼ cup ground flaxseeds
2 tablespoons sugar
½ teaspoon ground cinnamon
2 eggs, lightly beaten
2 egg whites
½ cup fat-free milk
1 tablespoon sugar
1 teaspoon vanilla
8 ounces hearty whole wheat bread
¾ cup apricot spreadable fruit
¼ cup water
3 tablespoons maple-flavor syrup

1. Preheat oven to 450°F. Coat a large baking sheet with cooking spray; set aside. In a shallow dish combine ground flaxseeds, the 2 tablespoons sugar, and the cinnamon; set aside. In a medium bowl combine eggs, egg whites, milk, the 1 tablespoon sugar, and the vanilla.

2. Cut bread into twelve 1-inch strips. Briefly dip bread strips into egg mixture, then roll in flaxseed mixture to coat. Place strips ½ inch apart on the prepared baking sheet. Bake for 12 to 15 minutes or until light brown and crisp.

3. Meanwhile, for apricot dipping sauce, in a small saucepan combine spreadable fruit, the water, and syrup. Bring to boiling; reduce heat. Simmer, uncovered, for 5 minutes. Cool slightly. Serve toast strips with sauce. **MAKES 6 SERVINGS**

Make-Ahead Directions:
Prepare as directed through Step 2. Cool toast strips completely. Place in an airtight container; cover. Freeze up to 1 month. To serve, preheat oven to 450°F. Place frozen toast strips on an ungreased baking sheet. Bake about 6 minutes or until heated through, turning once. Or place four frozen toast strips on a microwave-safe plate. Microwave on 100 percent power (high) about 30 seconds or until heated through. Prepare sauce as directed; serve with toast strips.

Berry Breakfast Pizzas

START TO FINISH: 25 minutes

NUTRITION FACTS PER PIZZA

Calories 343   *Fat* 14 g   *Cholesterol* 39 mg   *Sodium* 359 mg   *Carbohydrates* 51 g   *Fiber* 4 g   *Protein* 6 g

¼   cup granulated sugar
4   teaspoons cornstarch
    Dash salt
½   cup water
2   cups mixed fresh berries,
    such as blueberries,
    raspberries, and/or
    blackberries
1   teaspoon butter
1   teaspoon finely shredded
    orange peel
4   ounces reduced-fat cream
    cheese (Neufchâtel), softened
2   tablespoons orange
    marmalade
2   teaspoons granulated sugar
¼   teaspoon ground cardamom
2   pita bread rounds, split
2   tablespoons butter, melted
    Powdered sugar (optional)

1. For berry topping, in a medium saucepan combine ¼ cup granulated sugar, cornstarch, and salt. Stir in the water. Stir in ½ cup of the berries. Cook and stir over medium heat until thickened. Remove from heat. Add an additional 1 cup of the berries and the 1 teaspoon butter, stirring until butter is melted. Gently stir in orange peel.

2. In a medium mixing bowl combine cream cheese and orange marmalade; beat with an electric mixer on low to medium speed until smooth. In a small bowl stir together the 2 teaspoons granulated sugar and the cardamom.

3. Toast the split pita rounds. Brush pita rounds with the 2 tablespoons melted butter; sprinkle with the sugar-cardamom mixture. Spread cream cheese mixture on pita rounds. Spread berry topping on cream cheese mixture. Top with the remaining ½ cup berries. If desired, sprinkle with powdered sugar. **MAKES 4 PIZZAS**

Make-Ahead Directions:
Prepare the berry topping as directed in Step 1 and cool completely. Cover and chill for 2 to 8 hours.

Maple-Pecan Breakfast Porridge

START TO FINISH: 25 minutes

2½ cups water
¼ teaspoon salt
1 cup cracked wheat
1 large cooking apple, such as Rome Beauty, Jonathan, or Braeburn; chopped
2 to 3 tablespoons pure maple syrup
1 teaspoon ground cinnamon
3 tablespoons chopped pecans, toasted (see tip, page 15)
Vanilla low-fat yogurt (optional)
Ground cinnamon (optional)

1. In a medium saucepan bring the water and salt to boiling; stir in cracked wheat. Return to boiling; reduce heat. Simmer, covered, for 10 minutes. Stir in apple. Return to boiling; reduce heat. Simmer, covered, for 2 to 5 minutes more or until cracked wheat is tender. Remove from heat. Let stand, covered, for 5 minutes.

2. Stir maple syrup and the 1 teaspoon cinnamon into the porridge. Divide porridge among four serving bowls. Sprinkle with pecans. If desired, top with yogurt and sprinkle with additional cinnamon. **MAKES 4 SERVINGS**

Pumpkin-Apple Quick Oatmeal

START TO FINISH: 15 minutes

NUTRITION FACTS PER SERVING

Calories 168
Fat 2 g
Cholesterol 1 mg
Sodium 30 mg
Carbohydrates 35 g
Fiber 4 g
Protein 5 g

1⅓ cups water
⅔   cup apple juice or apple cider
½   cup canned pumpkin
⅓   cup snipped dried apples
1¼ cups quick-cooking rolled oats
1   tablespoon packed brown
     sugar
1   teaspoon ground cinnamon
¼   teaspoon ground nutmeg
½   cup plain fat-free yogurt
     Ground cinnamon (optional)
     Honey (optional)
     Pumpkin seeds (pepitas)
     (optional)

1. In a medium saucepan combine the water, apple juice, pumpkin, and dried apples. Bring to boiling. Meanwhile, in a small bowl stir together oats, brown sugar, the 1 teaspoon cinnamon, and the nutmeg. Stir oats mixture into boiling pumpkin mixture. Cook for 1 minute, stirring occasionally.

2. Divide oatmeal among four serving bowls. Top with yogurt. If desired, serve with additional cinnamon, honey, and pumpkin seeds. **MAKES 4 SERVINGS**

Peanut Butter and Fruit Quinoa

PREP: 10 minutes
COOK: 15 minutes

NUTRITION FACTS PER SERVING

Calories 290   *Fat* 9 g   *Cholesterol* 0 mg   *Sodium* 89 mg   *Carbohydrates* 44 g   *Fiber* 5 g   *Protein* 10 g

2   cups water
1   cup uncooked quinoa, rinsed and drained
¼   cup apple juice
3   tablespoons reduced-fat creamy peanut butter
1   small banana, chopped
2   tablespoons raspberry or strawberry spreadable fruit
4   teaspoons unsalted peanuts
    Fat-free milk (optional)

1. In a medium saucepan bring the water to boiling; stir in quinoa. Return to boiling; reduce heat. Simmer, covered, about 15 minutes or until water is absorbed. Remove from heat. Stir in apple juice and peanut butter until combined. Stir in banana.

2. Divide quinoa among four serving bowls. Top with spreadable fruit and peanuts. If desired, serve with milk. **MAKES 4 SERVINGS**

Almond Breakfast Risotto with Dried Fruit

PREP: 10 minutes
COOK: 20 minutes

NUTRITION FACTS PER SERVING

Calories 258
Fat 3 g
Cholesterol 4 mg
Sodium 227 mg
Carbohydrates 50 g
Fiber 2 g
Protein 10 g

1   cup water
⅔   cup Arborio rice
¼   teaspoon salt
⅓   cup dried cherries
¼   cup coarsely chopped dried apricots
3   cups fat-free milk
½   teaspoon ground cinnamon
½   teaspoon almond extract
¼   cup sliced almonds, toasted (see tip, page 15)

1. In a medium saucepan bring the water to boiling over medium-high heat. Stir in rice and salt. Cook, uncovered, for 5 to 6 minutes or until water is absorbed, stirring occasionally. Stir in dried cherries and apricots.

2. Meanwhile, pour milk into a 4-cup microwave-safe liquid measuring cup or medium bowl; microwave on 100 percent (high) power for 2 minutes. Stir in cinnamon.

3. Add the hot milk mixture, ½ cup at a time, to the rice mixture, stirring until liquid is absorbed (20 to 25 minutes total). Remove from heat. Stir in almond extract. Sprinkle with toasted almonds.
MAKES 4 SERVINGS

French Toast Bread Pudding

PREP: 15 minutes
CHILL: 4 hours
SLOW COOK: 7 hours (low)
COOL: 30 minutes

NUTRITION FACTS PER SERVING

Calories 231
Fat 5 g
Cholesterol 33 mg
Sodium 287 mg
Carbohydrates 39 g
Fiber 1 g
Protein 7 g

Disposable slow cooker liner
12 ounces challah or sweet bread (such as Portuguese or Hawaiian sweet bread), cut into 1-inch cubes (about 9 cups)
4 cups fat-free milk
½ cup sugar
3 eggs or ¾ cup refrigerated or frozen egg product, thawed
1 teaspoon vanilla
¼ teaspoon salt
Sugar-free caramel ice cream topping, warmed

1. Place the disposable liner in a 3½- or 4-quart slow cooker with removable ceramic pot. Place bread cubes in prepared slow cooker.

2. In a large bowl whisk together milk, sugar, eggs, vanilla, and salt. Pour over bread cubes in cooker. Lightly press bread down with the back of a large spoon to moisten bread completely. Cover ceramic pot and refrigerate for 4 to 24 hours.

3. Cover and cook on low-heat setting for 7 to 8 hours or until a knife inserted in the center comes out clean. Turn off cooker. If possible, remove ceramic pot from cooker. Cool for 30 minutes.

4. To serve, carefully lift disposable liner from cooker. Using a plate, transfer pudding to a cutting board; slice French toast. (If desired, spoon pudding into serving dishes.) Top with ice cream topping. **MAKES 12 SERVINGS**

Spiced Bran Muffins with Dried Apricots

PREP: 25 minutes   BAKE: 20 minutes   COOL: 5 minutes
OVEN: 400°F

NUTRITION FACTS PER MUFFIN

Calories 130   *Fat* 3 g   *Cholesterol* 1 mg   *Sodium* 215 mg   *Carbohydrates* 27 g   *Fiber* 6 g   *Protein* 4 g

Nonstick cooking spray (optional)
3   cups whole bran cereal (not flakes)
1   cup boiling water
2½ cups white whole wheat flour
½   cup packed brown sugar
2   teaspoons baking powder
1   teaspoon ground cinnamon
1   teaspoon ground ginger
¼   teaspoon cloves
½   teaspoon baking soda
½   teaspoon salt
2   cups buttermilk
1   very ripe banana, mashed (¾ cup)
½   cup refrigerated or frozen egg product, thawed, or 2 eggs, lightly beaten
¼   cup canola oil
½   cup snipped dried apricots

1. Preheat oven to 400°F. Grease twenty-four 2½-inch muffin cups or line with paper bake cups; set aside. Spray paper cups, if using, with cooking spray. Place bran cereal in a medium bowl. Pour boiling water over cereal. Stir to moisten cereal; set aside.

2. In another medium bowl combine flour, brown sugar, baking powder, cinnamon, ginger, cloves, baking soda, and salt. In a large bowl combine buttermilk, banana, egg product, and oil. Stir cereal and flour mixtures into buttermilk mixture just until moistened. Stir in apricots.

3. Spoon batter into prepared muffin cups, filling each three-fourths full. Bake about 20 minutes or until a wooden toothpick inserted in centers comes out clean. Cool in muffin cups on a wire rack for 5 minutes. Remove from muffin cups; serve warm.
MAKES 24 MUFFINS

Snickerdoodle Crescent Rolls

PREP: 30 minutes
RISE: 1 hour 30 minutes
BAKE: 15 minutes
OVEN: 350°F

NUTRITION FACTS PER SERVING

Calories 130
Fat 3 g
Cholesterol 8 mg
Sodium 91 mg
Carbohydrates 22 g
Fiber 2 g
Protein 4 g

1   to 1½ cups all-purpose flour
1   package active dry yeast
¾   cup fat-free milk
2   tablespoons packed brown sugar
2   tablespoons butter
¼   teaspoon salt
¼   cup refrigerated or frozen egg product, thawed, or 1 egg, lightly beaten
1   cup whole wheat flour
1   tablespoon butter, softened
3   tablespoons granulated sugar
2   teaspoons ground cinnamon
1   egg white
1   tablespoon water

1. In a large mixing bowl stir together 1 cup of the all-purpose flour and the yeast. In a small saucepan heat and stir milk, brown sugar, 2 tablespoons butter, and salt just until warm (120°F to 130°F); add to flour mixture along with egg. Beat with an electric mixer on low for 30 seconds, scraping sides of bowl constantly. Beat on high for 3 minutes. Using a wooden spoon, stir in whole wheat flour and as much of the remaining all-purpose flour as you can.

2. Turn dough out onto a lightly floured surface. Knead in enough remaining all-purpose flour to make a slightly soft dough that is smooth and elastic (3 to 5 minutes total). Shape dough into a ball. Place in a lightly greased bowl; turn once to grease surface. Cover and let rise in a warm place until double in size (about 1 hour).

3. Punch dough down. Divide dough in half. Cover and let rest for 10 minutes. Line a large baking sheet with parchment paper or lightly coat with nonstick cooking spray; set aside. On a lightly floured surface roll each dough half into a 12-inch circle. Evenly spread the 1 tablespoon butter on both circles. In a small bowl stir together the granulated sugar and cinnamon; evenly sprinkle 1 tablespoon cinnamon-sugar over each circle. Cut each circle into 6 wedges.

4. To shape rolls, begin at wide end of each wedge and loosely roll toward the point. Place, point sides down, 2 to 3 inches apart on prepared baking sheet, then curve ends of each in a crescent shape. Cover; let rise in a warm place until nearly double in size (about 30 minutes). In a small bowl beat together 1 egg white and the 1 tablespoon water. Brush evenly over the rolls, then sprinkle with remaining cinnamon-sugar.

5. Preheat oven to 350°F. Bake about 15 minutes or until golden. Transfer rolls to a wire rack; cool slightly; serve warm.
MAKES 12 SERVINGS

Bacon, Cheddar, and Tomato Rosti

PREP: 15 minutes
COOK: 14 minutes

NUTRITION FACTS PER SERVING

Calories 208
Fat 7 g
Cholesterol 63 mg
Sodium 374 mg
Carbohydrates 26 g
Fiber 4 g
Protein 10 g

1   egg
1   egg white
1   medium zucchini, shredded (about 1½ cups)
2   slices packaged ready-to-serve cooked bacon, crumbled
1   teaspoon snipped fresh oregano
¼   teaspoon salt
¼   teaspoon ground black pepper
4   cups frozen shredded or diced hash brown potatoes with onions and peppers
2   teaspoons canola oil
½   cup shredded reduced-fat cheddar cheese (2 ounces)
1   cup halved or quartered cherry tomatoes
     Fresh oregano sprigs

1. In a large bowl beat together whole egg and egg white. Stir in zucchini, bacon, the 1 teaspoon oregano, the salt, and pepper. Stir in frozen hash brown potatoes.

2. In a large nonstick skillet heat oil over medium heat. Evenly spread potato mixture in skillet. Cook for 8 to 10 minutes or until bottom is browned. Using the edge of a nonmetal spatula, cut rosti into quarters. Carefully flip each quarter.* Sprinkle with cheese. Cook about 6 minutes more or until browned on bottom. Serve topped with tomatoes and additional oregano.

*Tip: If using diced potatoes, the rosti might fall apart when you try to flip the quarters. If desired, transfer the quarters to a baking sheet and broil 4 to 5 inches from the heat for 1 to 2 minutes or until tops are firm and starting to brown. Sprinkle with cheese; broil about 1 minute more or until cheese is melted. Serve topped with tomatoes and additional oregano.
MAKES 4 SERVINGS

Spanish Eggs

START TO FINISH: 30 minutes

NUTRITION FACTS PER SERVING

Calories 176   *Fat* 10 g   *Cholesterol* 191 mg   *Sodium* 395 mg   *Carbohydrates* 13 g   *Fiber* 3 g   *Protein* 11 g

1   tablespoon olive oil
½   cup chopped onion
       (1 medium)
1   small fresh Anaheim chile
       pepper, stemmed, seeded, and
       chopped*
1   clove garlic, minced
4   large tomatoes, chopped
1   small zucchini, halved
       lengthwise and thinly sliced
1   teaspoon dried savory or
       cilantro, crushed
½   teaspoon salt
4   eggs
½   cup crumbled queso fresco
       Fresh cilantro sprigs
       (optional)
       Corn tortillas, warmed
       (optional)

1. In a large skillet heat olive oil over medium heat. Add onion, Anaheim chile, and garlic; cook about 5 minutes or until tender. Add tomatoes, zucchini, savory, and salt; cook about 5 minutes or until tomatoes release their liquid and zucchini is tender.

2. One at a time, break eggs into a custard cup. Carefully slide egg into the tomato mixture, allowing each egg an equal amount of space. Simmer, covered, over medium-low heat for 3 to 5 minutes or until whites are completely set and yolks begin to thicken but are not hard. Sprinkle with queso fresco. If desired, garnish with fresh cilantro and serve with warm corn tortillas.

MAKES 4 SERVINGS

*Tip: Because chile peppers contain volatile oils that can burn your skin and eyes, avoid direct contact with them as much as possible. When working with chile peppers, wear plastic or rubber gloves. If your bare hands do touch the peppers, wash your hands and nails well with soap and warm water.

Ranchero Eggs over Polenta

START TO FINISH: 30 minutes

NUTRITION FACTS PER SERVING

Calories 230
Fat 5 g
Cholesterol 212 mg
Sodium 897 mg
Carbohydrates 33 g
Fiber 6 g
Protein 13 g

Nonstick cooking spray
1 16-ounce tube refrigerated cooked polenta, cut crosswise into 8 slices
1 10-ounce can diced tomatoes and green chiles, undrained
3 tablespoons tomato paste
¾ cup no-salt-added canned black beans
2 teaspoons vinegar
4 eggs
2 tablespoons snipped fresh cilantro
Freshly ground black pepper (optional)

1. Coat a large nonstick skillet with cooking spray; heat over medium-high heat. Cook polenta slices in hot skillet about 6 minutes or until golden brown, turning once halfway through cooking time. Meanwhile, for sauce, in a medium microwave-safe bowl stir together tomatoes and tomato paste. Stir in black beans. Cover; microwave on 100 percent (high) power about 2 minutes or until hot. Set aside.

2. To poach eggs, grease a large skillet; add water to reach 1½ to 2 inches up the sides of the skillet. Bring water almost to boiling over medium-high heat. Stir in vinegar. Reduce heat until gently simmering. Break eggs, one at a time, into a small bowl or cup; gently slip each egg into the simmering water. Poach eggs for 4 to 6 minutes or until desired doneness, spooning water over eggs the last half of cooking time. Remove eggs with a slotted spoon.

3. To serve, place two slices of fried polenta on each of four serving plates. Ladle one-fourth of the sauce over each serving. Top each with a poached egg and some of the cilantro. If desired, sprinkle with pepper. **MAKES 4 SERVINGS**

Mediterranean Breakfast Sandwiches

START TO FINISH: 20 minutes
OVEN: 375°F

NUTRITION FACTS PER SANDWICH

Calories 242
Fat 12 g
Cholesterol 214 mg
Sodium 501 mg
Carbohydrates 25 g
Fiber 6 g
Protein 13 g

4	multigrain sandwich thins
4	teaspoons olive oil
1	tablespoon snipped fresh rosemary or ½ teaspoon dried rosemary, crushed
4	eggs
2	cups fresh baby spinach leaves
1	medium tomato, cut into 8 thin slices
4	tablespoons reduced-fat feta cheese
⅛	teaspoon kosher salt Freshly ground black pepper

1. Preheat oven to 375°F. Split sandwich thins. Place on a baking sheet; brush cut sides with 2 teaspoons of the olive oil. Bake about 5 minutes or until edges are light brown and crisp.

2. Meanwhile, in a large skillet heat the remaining 2 teaspoons olive oil and the rosemary over medium-high heat. Break eggs, one at a time, into skillet. Cook about 1 minute or until whites are set but yolks are still runny. Break yolks with a spatula. Flip eggs; cook other side until done. Remove from heat.

3. Place the bottom halves of the toasted sandwich thins on four serving plates. Divide spinach among sandwich thins on plates. Top each with two tomato slices, an egg, and 1 tablespoon of the feta cheese. Sprinkle with salt and pepper. Top with the sandwich thin tops. **MAKES 4 SANDWICHES**

Fried Egg Toast with Tomatoes

START TO FINISH: 20 minutes

NUTRITION FACTS PER SERVING

Calories 177   *Fat* 9 g   *Cholesterol* 188 mg   *Sodium* 225 mg   *Carbohydrates* 13 g   *Fiber* 2 g   *Protein* 11 g

4   slices whole grain sandwich bread
2   teaspoons olive oil
4   eggs
¾   cup chopped tomatoes
2   teaspoons chopped green onions or snipped fresh parsley, oregano, and/or thyme (optional)
2   tablespoons finely shredded Parmesan cheese

1. Using a 2½-inch round cookie cutter, cut a hole from the center of each bread slice. In an extra-large nonstick skillet heat oil over medium-high heat. Add bread slices; cook about 1 minute or until lightly toasted. Turn bread over.

2. One at a time, break an egg into a cup, taking care not to break the yolk. Hold the lip of the cup as close to the hole in one of the bread slices as possible and slip egg into hole. Reduce heat to medium. Cook, covered, for 5 to 6 minutes or until whites are completely set and yolks begin to thicken.

3. Transfer egg toasts to serving plates. Top with tomatoes and, if desired, green onions. Sprinkle with cheese. **MAKES 4 SERVINGS**

Chile-Quinoa Breakfast Burritos

START TO FINISH: 30 minutes

NUTRITION FACTS PER BURRITO

Calories 342
Fat 10 g
Cholesterol 106 mg
Sodium 1,042 mg
Carbohydrates 51 g
Fiber 9 g
Protein 17 g

1   cup water
½   cup uncooked quinoa, rinsed and drained
¼   cup salsa
2   eggs
2   egg whites
2   tablespoons low-fat milk
⅛   teaspoon salt
    Nonstick cooking spray
¼   cup shredded reduced-fat Mexican-style four cheese blend (1 ounce)
4   10-inch multigrain tortillas
1   7-ounce can whole green chile peppers, drained
    Chopped fresh tomato (optional)
    Snipped fresh cilantro (optional)

1. In a small saucepan combine the water and quinoa. Bring to boiling; reduce heat to medium-low. Cook, covered, for 10 to 15 minutes or until water is absorbed. Remove from heat. Stir in salsa.

2. Meanwhile, in a small bowl use a fork to beat together whole eggs and egg whites. Beat in milk and salt. Coat a medium nonstick skillet with cooking spray; heat skillet over medium heat. Pour egg mixture into hot skillet. As eggs begin to set, fold mixture over on itself, continuing to fold until fully cooked. Cut egg mixture into four portions in skillet; top each with 1 tablespoon of the cheese. Remove from heat.

3. Place a tortilla on each of four serving plates. Lay chile peppers to cover half of each tortilla. Top chile peppers with quinoa mixture. Top with eggs. If desired, garnish with tomatoes and/or cilantro. Roll or fold tortillas. If desired, toast burritos in a large dry skillet over medium heat until light brown and crisp. **MAKES 4 BURRITOS**

Hearty Breakfast Tacos

PREP: 20 minutes
BAKE: 7 minutes
OVEN: 375°F

NUTRITION FACTS PER 2 TACOS

Calories 238
Fat 8 g
Cholesterol 191 mg
Sodium 498 mg
Carbohydrates 28 g
Fiber 3 g
Protein 14 g

8   6-inch corn tortillas
1   teaspoon vegetable oil
¼   teaspoon salt
     Nonstick cooking spray
1   cup frozen shredded hash brown potatoes
2   tablespoons chopped green sweet pepper
4   eggs, lightly beaten
2   egg whites
5   tablespoons salsa
½   cup canned reduced-sodium black beans, drained and rinsed
¼   cup shredded reduced-fat cheddar cheese (1 ounce)
     Lime wedges (optional)
     Salsa (optional)

1. Position oven rack in center of oven. Preheat oven to 375°F. Stack tortillas and wrap in damp paper towels. Microwave on 100 percent power (high) about 40 seconds or until warm and softened. Lightly brush both sides of tortillas with oil; sprinkle with salt. Slide oven rack out slightly. Carefully drape each tortilla over two bars of oven rack, forming shells with flat bottoms (sides will drape more during baking). Bake about 7 minutes or until crisp. Using tongs, transfer warm shells to a plate.

2. Meanwhile, lightly coat a large nonstick skillet with cooking spray; heat skillet over medium-high heat. Add hash brown potatoes and sweet pepper; cook for 2 to 3 minutes or until potatoes are lightly browned, stirring occasionally. Reduce heat to medium. In a small bowl combine eggs, egg whites, and 1 tablespoon of the salsa. Pour over potatoes in skillet. Cook, without stirring, until mixture begins to set on the bottom and around edges. Using a spatula or large spoon, lift and fold the partially cooked egg mixture so the uncooked portion flows underneath. Continue cooking over medium heat for 2 to 3 minutes or until egg mixture is cooked through but still glossy and moist. Immediately remove from heat.

3. Spoon egg mixture into tortilla shells. Top with beans and the remaining salsa; sprinkle with cheese. If desired, serve with lime wedges and additional salsa.
MAKES 8 TACOS

Make-Ahead Directions:
Prepare as directed in Step 1, except cool shells completely on oven rack. Wrap in foil and store at room temperature up to 24 hours. Continue as directed.

Greens and Bacon Omelet Wraps

START TO FINISH: 25 minutes

NUTRITION FACTS PER WRAP

Calories 216
Fat 9 g
Cholesterol 192 mg
Sodium 597 mg
Carbohydrates 24 g
Fiber 13 g
Protein 22 g

2 slices turkey bacon
   Nonstick cooking spray
⅓ cup chopped red sweet pepper
¼ cup sliced green onions (2)
2 cups coarsely chopped, stemmed fresh kale
4 eggs, lightly beaten
2 egg whites
½ cup low-fat cottage cheese
½ teaspoon dried Italian seasoning, crushed
¼ teaspoon freshly ground black pepper
4 10-inch low-fat, high-fiber whole grain flour tortillas, warmed

1. Coat a large skillet with cooking spray. Cook bacon in skillet until crisp. Remove bacon from skillet. Cool and chop; set aside.

2. Coat the same skillet with cooking spray; heat skillet over medium heat. Add sweet pepper and green onions; cook about 2 minutes or until tender, stirring occasionally. Add kale; cook and stir for 2 to 3 minutes more or until kale begins to wilt.

3. In a medium bowl combine eggs, egg whites, cottage cheese, Italian seasoning, black pepper, and the chopped bacon. Pour egg mixture over vegetables in skillet. Cook over medium heat. As mixture sets, run a spatula around edges of skillet, lifting egg mixture so the uncooked portion flows underneath. Continue cooking and lifting edges just until set. Slide omelet from skillet onto a cutting board; cut into quarters.

4. For each wrap, place an omelet portion in the center of each tortilla. Fold in opposite sides; roll up. If desired, secure with wooden skewers. **MAKES 4 WRAPS**

CHAPTER 3

Sandwiches

Avocado BLT Sandwiches

START TO FINISH: 25 minutes

NUTRITION FACTS
PER SANDWICH

Calories 257
Fat 14 g
Cholesterol 10 mg
Sodium 432 mg
Carbohydrates 27 g
Fiber 7 g
Protein 9 g

1   ripe avocado
2   tablespoons light mayonnaise or salad dressing
1   teaspoon lemon juice
1   clove garlic, minced
4   slices bacon, crisp-cooked and halved crosswise
4   leaves romaine lettuce
1   medium tomato, thinly sliced
8   slices whole wheat bread, toasted

1. Halve, seed, and peel avocado. Transfer one avocado half to a small bowl; mash with a potato masher or the back of a wooden spoon. Stir in mayonnaise, lemon juice, and garlic; set aside. Thinly slice the remaining avocado half.

2. Arrange avocado slices, bacon, lettuce, and tomato on four of the bread slices. Spread the mashed avocado mixture on the remaining four bread slices; place on top of the filled bread slices, spread sides down. **MAKES 4 SANDWICHES**

Garden Beef Burgers

PREP: 15 minutes
GRILL: 14 minutes

NUTRITION FACTS PER BURGER

Calories 258
Fat 10 g
Cholesterol 55 mg
Sodium 229 mg
Carbohydrates 19 g
Fiber 3 g
Protein 21 g

1   egg white, lightly beaten
½   cup shredded carrot
     (1 medium)
¼   cup thinly sliced green
     onions (2)
¼   cup shredded zucchini
2   cloves garlic, minced
⅛   teaspoon ground black pepper
12 ounces lean ground beef
8   ½-inch slices whole wheat
     baguette-style French bread,
     toasted
¾   cup fresh spinach
1   medium tomato, thinly sliced
½   cup thinly shaved zucchini
     ribbons*

1. In a large bowl combine egg white, carrot, green onions, shredded zucchini, garlic, and pepper. Add ground beef; mix well. Shape meat mixture into four ¾-inch-thick patties.

2. For a charcoal or gas grill, place patties on the grill rack directly over medium heat. Cover and grill for 14 to 18 minutes or until patties are done (160°F), turning once.

3. Serve each patty between two toasted bread slices with spinach, tomato, and shaved zucchini.
MAKES 4 BURGERS

***Tip:** To make zucchini ribbons, use a vegetable peeler to thinly shave along the length of the zucchini.

Greek Feta Burgers

PREP: 20 minutes
COOK: 8 minutes

NUTRITION FACTS PER BURGER

Calories 292   *Fat* 14 g   *Cholesterol* 79 mg   *Sodium* 356 mg   *Carbohydrates* 14 g   *Fiber* 2 g   *Protein* 27 g

8   ounces lean ground beef
1   tablespoon crumbled reduced-
    fat feta cheese
1½ teaspoons snipped fresh
    Italian (flat-leaf) parsley
⅛   teaspoon ground black pepper
1   clove garlic, minced
1   whole wheat hamburger bun,
    split and toasted
½   cup fresh spinach leaves
2   tomato slices
1   recipe Cucumber Sauce
    Thin red onion slices
    (optional)

1. In a medium bowl combine ground beef, feta cheese, parsley, pepper, and garlic. Shape mixture into two ½-inch-thick patties.

2. In a large nonstick skillet cook patties over medium-high heat for 8 to 10 minutes or until an instant-read thermometer inserted into sides of patties registers 160°F,* turning once.

3. Line cut sides of bun halves with spinach. Top with patties, tomato slices, and Cucumber Sauce. If desired, garnish with red onion.
MAKES 2 BURGERS

Cucumber Sauce: In a small bowl combine 3 tablespoons chopped, seeded cucumber; 2 tablespoons light sour cream; 1 clove garlic, minced; ½ teaspoon snipped fresh Italian (flat-leaf) parsley; ¼ teaspoon snipped fresh mint; and ⅛ teaspoon sea salt. Makes about ¼ cup.

***Tip:** The internal color of a burger is not a reliable doneness indicator. A beef or pork burger cooked to 160°F is safe, regardless of color. To test for doneness, insert an instant-read thermometer through the side of the burger to a depth of 2 to 3 inches.

Mu Shu Chicken Wraps

START TO FINISH: 25 minutes
OVEN: 350°F

NUTRITION FACTS PER SERVING

Calories 294
Fat 7 g
Cholesterol 50 mg
Sodium 574 mg
Carbohydrates 2 g
Fiber 12 g
Protein 30 g

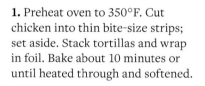

12	ounces skinless, boneless chicken breast halves
4	whole grain tortillas
2	teaspoons canola oil or olive oil
2	cups small broccoli florets
1	onion, chopped
½	teaspoon ground ginger
¼	teaspoon ground black pepper
3	tablespoons bottled hoisin sauce

1. Preheat oven to 350°F. Cut chicken into thin bite-size strips; set aside. Stack tortillas and wrap in foil. Bake about 10 minutes or until heated through and softened.

2. Meanwhile, in a large nonstick skillet heat 1 teaspoon of the oil over medium-high heat. Add broccoli, onion, ginger, and pepper. Cook and stir for 3 to 5 minutes or just until vegetables are tender; remove vegetable mixture from skillet. Add chicken and the remaining 1 teaspoon oil. Cook for 3 to 5 minutes or until chicken is no longer pink, stirring occasionally. Add vegetable mixture and hoisin sauce to chicken mixture. Heat through.

3. To assemble, use a slotted spoon to place about ¾ cup of mu shu filling on one side of each tortilla. Roll up tortillas; cut in half to serve. If desired, serve skillet juices as dipping sauce.
MAKES 4 SERVINGS

Rotisserie Chicken Banh Mi

PREP: 25 minutes
BAKE: 5 minutes
OVEN: 425°F

⅓   cup white vinegar
¼   cup sugar
⅛   teaspoon salt
1   cup shredded carrots
    (2 medium)
¼   cup light mayonnaise or salad
    dressing
1   to 2 teaspoons Asian chili
    sauce (Sriracha sauce)
½   teaspoon reduced-sodium soy
    sauce
⅛   teaspoon sugar
1   8-ounce loaf baguette-
    style French bread, split
    horizontally and each cut in
    half for 4 pieces
8   ounces sliced purchased
    roasted chicken breast
⅓   of a long seedless (English)
    cucumber, thinly sliced
    in narrow strips (about
    3 ounces)
1   fresh jalapeño chile pepper,
    thinly sliced (see tip, page 42)
    (optional)
⅓   cup fresh cilantro leaves

1. Preheat oven to 425°F. In a small bowl combine the vinegar, the ¼ cup sugar, and salt, stirring until sugar is dissolved. Add carrots; toss gently to coat. Let stand for 15 minutes.

2. Meanwhile, in another small bowl combine mayonnaise, Asian chili sauce, soy sauce, and the ⅛ teaspoon sugar.

3. Place bread halves, cut sides up, on rack in oven. Lightly toast about 5 minutes or just until warm.

Spread mayonnaise mixture on bread; top with chicken. Drain carrots; pat dry with paper towels. Arrange carrots on chicken. Top with cucumber and, if desired, jalapeño pepper. Sprinkle with cilantro leaves. **MAKES 4 SANDWICHES**

Sloppy Turkey and Veggie Sandwiches

START TO FINISH: 25 minutes

NUTRITION FACTS PER SANDWICH

Calories 263   *Fat* 5 g   *Cholesterol* 27 mg   *Sodium* 392 mg   *Carbohydrates* 32 g   *Fiber* 7 g   *Protein* 21 g

8   ounces uncooked ground turkey breast
2   cups chopped fresh cremini or button mushrooms
¾   cup chopped yellow or green sweet pepper (1 medium)
½   cup chopped onion (1 medium)
1   14.5-ounce can no-salt-added diced tomatoes with basil, garlic, and oregano, undrained
6   whole wheat hamburger buns, split and toasted
1   recipe Goat Cheese-Yogurt Sauce

1. In a large nonstick skillet cook turkey, mushrooms, sweet pepper, and onion over medium heat until turkey is brown and vegetables are tender, using a wooden spoon to break up meat as it cooks. Stir in tomatoes. Cook over medium-low heat for 5 minutes to blend flavors, stirring occasionally.

2. Divide turkey mixture among bun bottoms. Spoon Goat Cheese-Yogurt Sauce on meat mixture. Add bun tops. **MAKES 6 SANDWICHES**

Goat Cheese-Yogurt Sauce: In a small bowl combine 4 ounces goat cheese (chèvre), softened; ¼ cup snipped fresh chives; 1 clove garlic, minced; ⅛ teaspoon salt; and ⅛ teaspoon ground black pepper. Gradually stir in one 6-ounce container plain fat-free Greek yogurt until smooth. Makes about 1¼ cups.

Grilled Fajita Burgers

PREP: 20 minutes
GRILL: 10 minutes

NUTRITION FACTS PER SERVING

Calories 285
Fat 10 g
Cholesterol 55 mg
Sodium 430 mg
Carbohydrates 20 g
Fiber 5 g
Protein 29 g

8 ounces uncooked ground turkey breast or 90% or higher lean ground beef
¼ cup purchased salsa
¼ teaspoon ground cumin
⅛ teaspoon ground black pepper
Dash salt
½ cup thinly sliced sweet onion (such as Vidalia or Maui Maui)
½ of a medium red sweet pepper, thinly sliced (½ cup)
1 teaspoon canola oil
2 purchased tostada shells
¼ of a medium avocado, seeded, peeled, and sliced or chopped

1. In a medium bowl combine turkey, salsa, cumin, black pepper, and salt. Mix well. Shape into two ½-inch-thick patties. Fold a 24×12-inch piece of heavy-duty foil in half to make a 12-inch square. Place onion and sweet pepper in center of foil; drizzle with oil. Bring up two opposite edges of foil and seal with a double fold. Fold remaining edges together to completely enclose the vegetables, leaving space for steam to build.*

2. For a charcoal grill, place vegetable packet and patties on the rack of an uncovered grill directly over medium heat. Grill for 10 to 13 minutes or until an instant-read thermometer inserted into the side of each patty registers 165°F for turkey or 160°F for beef and vegetables are tender, turning once halfway through grilling. (For a gas grill, preheat grill. Reduce heat to medium. Place packet and patties on grill rack over heat. Cover and grill as directed.)

3. Serve grilled patties on tostada shells. Top with vegetables and avocado. MAKES 2 SERVINGS

*Tip: The onion and pepper with oil may be cooked in a skillet on the side burner of the grill or on the stove top. In a covered medium skillet cook onion and red pepper slices in hot oil over medium heat for 10 minutes, stirring occasionally. Uncover and cook about 3 minutes more or until pepper is very tender and onion is golden brown, stirring occasionally.

Caesar Salad Burgers

START TO FINISH: 20 minutes

NUTRITION FACTS PER BURGER

Calories 368
Fat 14 g
Cholesterol 87 mg
Sodium 797 mg
Carbohydrates 33 g
Fiber 2 g
Protein 26 g

1   pound uncooked ground turkey breast
2   tablespoons Worcestershire-style marinade for chicken
¼ to ½ teaspoon ground black pepper
⅓ cup bottled light Caesar salad dressing
1   teaspoon finely shredded lemon peel
4   whole grain ciabatta buns, split and toasted
2   leaves romaine lettuce, trimmed and torn into 8 pieces
4   thin slices red onion (optional)
4   slices tomato (optional)

1. In a large bowl combine ground turkey, Worcestershire-style marinade, and pepper. Shape mixture into four ½-inch-thick patties. Heat a lightly greased grill pan over medium-high heat. Place patties in hot pan. Cook for 10 to 12 minutes or until done (165°F),* turning once halfway through cooking. If patties brown too quickly, reduce heat to medium.

2. Meanwhile, in a small bowl combine salad dressing and lemon peel. Spread about half of the dressing mixture on bottoms of buns. Place burgers on buns. If desired, top with lettuce, onion, tomato, and remaining dressing. Add bun tops. **MAKES 4 BURGERS**

*Tip: The internal color of a burger is not a reliable doneness indicator. A chicken or turkey burger cooked to 165°F is safe, regardless of color. To test for doneness, insert an instant-read thermometer through the side of the burger to a depth of 2 to 3 inches.

Greek-Style Turkey Burgers

PREP: 15 minutes
GRILL: 14 minutes

NUTRITION FACTS PER BURGER

Calories 275   *Fat* 6 g   *Cholesterol* 53 mg   *Sodium* 507 mg   *Carbohydrates* 23 g   *Fiber* 4 g   *Protein* 35 g

1 egg white, lightly beaten
⅓ cup fine dry whole wheat bread crumbs*
1 tablespoon plain low-fat yogurt
1 teaspoon snipped fresh rosemary or ½ teaspoon dried rosemary, crushed
1 teaspoon snipped fresh oregano or ½ teaspoon dried oregano, crushed
1 tablespoon crumbled feta cheese
⅛ teaspoon ground black pepper
1 pound uncooked ground turkey breast or chicken breast
   Mixed torn greens (optional)
1 recipe Olive-Tomato Salsa
¼ cup crumbled feta cheese (1 ounce)
   Plain low-fat yogurt (optional)
2 whole wheat pita bread rounds, halved and lightly toasted

1. In a medium bowl combine egg white, bread crumbs, the 1 tablespoon yogurt, rosemary, oregano, the 1 tablespoon feta cheese, and pepper. Add turkey; mix well. Shape turkey mixture into four ¾-inch-thick patties.

2. For a charcoal or gas grill, grill patties on the rack of a covered grill directly over medium heat for 14 to 18 minutes or until no longer pink (165°F),** turning once halfway through grilling.

3. If desired, divide greens among four serving plates; top with patties. Top patties with Olive-Tomato Salsa, the ¼ cup feta cheese, and, if desired, additional yogurt. Serve burgers with pita bread. **MAKES 4 BURGERS**

Olive-Tomato Salsa: In a small bowl stir together 1 cup chopped, seeded tomato; ¼ cup chopped, seeded cucumber; ¼ cup chopped pitted Kalamata or other ripe olives; ½ teaspoon snipped fresh rosemary or ¼ teaspoon dried rosemary, crushed; and ½ teaspoon snipped fresh oregano or ¼ teaspoon dried oregano, crushed. Makes about 1½ cups.

*Tip: For fine dry whole wheat bread crumbs, place 1 slice whole wheat bread, toasted, in a food processor. Cover and to form fine crumbs. Makes ⅓ cup.

**Tip: The internal color of a burger is not a reliable doneness indicator. A chicken or turkey burger cooked to 165°F is safe, regardless of color. To test for doneness of a burger, insert an instant-read thermometer through the side of the patty to a depth of 2 to 3 inches.

Turkey Pizza Burgers

PREP: 15 minutes
GRILL: 14 minutes

NUTRITION FACTS PER BURGER

Calories 351
Fat 9 g
Cholesterol 127 mg
Sodium 487 mg
Carbohydrates 28 g
Fiber 3 g
Protein 38 g

1   egg, lightly beaten, or ¼ cup refrigerated or frozen egg product, thawed
¼   cup quick-cooking rolled oats
4   teaspoons snipped fresh oregano
⅛   teaspoon salt
⅛   teaspoon ground black pepper
1   pound uncooked ground turkey breast
4   ½-ounce slices provolone cheese
½   cup low-sodium tomato pasta sauce
4   whole wheat hamburger buns, toasted

1. In a medium bowl combine egg, rolled oats, 2 teaspoons of the oregano, the salt, and pepper. Add ground turkey breast; mix well. Shape turkey mixture into four ¾-inch-thick patties.

2. For a charcoal or gas grill, place patties on the grill rack directly over medium coals. Cover and grill for 14 to 18 minutes or until done (165°F),* turning once halfway through grilling and topping each patty with a cheese slice for the last minute of grilling.

3. Meanwhile, in a small saucepan cook pasta sauce until heated though.

4. Place patties on the bottom halves of buns. Top with pasta sauce, the remaining 2 teaspoons oregano. Add bun tops.
MAKES 4 BURGERS

*Tip: The internal color of a burger is not a reliable doneness indicator. A turkey or chicken burger cooked to 165°F is safe, regardless of color. To check the doneness of a burger, insert an instant-read thermometer through the side of the patty to a depth of 2 to 3 inches.

Cajun Turkey Sandwich

START TO FINISH: 20 minutes

NUTRITION FACTS PER SERVING

Calories 194
Fat 7 g
Cholesterol 35 mg
Sodium 602 mg
Carbohydrates 18 g
Fiber 3 g
Protein 15 g

¼ cup light mayonnaise or salad dressing
1 teaspoon purchased salt-free Cajun seasoning or Homemade Salt-Free Cajun Seasoning
1 clove garlic, minced
8 very thin slices firm-texture whole wheat bread, toasted if desired
1 cup fresh spinach leaves
8 ounces packaged lower-sodium sliced cooked turkey breast
4 tomato slices
1 green sweet pepper or fresh poblano chile pepper, seeded and sliced (see tip, page 57)

1. In a small bowl stir together mayonnaise, Cajun seasoning, and garlic. Spread on one side of each bread slice.

2. To assemble, layer four bread slices, spread sides up, with spinach, turkey, tomato slices, and sweet pepper or chile pepper. Top with remaining bread slices, spread sides down. Cut in half to serve.
MAKES 4 SERVINGS

Homemade Salt-Free Cajun Seasoning: In a small bowl stir together ¼ teaspoon white pepper, ¼ teaspoon garlic powder, ¼ teaspoon onion powder, ¼ teaspoon paprika, ¼ teaspoon ground black pepper, and ⅛ to ¼ teaspoon cayenne pepper.

Caprese Panini

START TO FINISH: 25 minutes

NUTRITION FACTS PER SANDWICH

Calories 216   *Fat* 8 g   *Cholesterol* 20 mg   *Sodium* 324 mg   *Carbohydrates* 23 g   *Fiber* 4 g   *Protein* 12 g

8   slices whole wheat bread
     Nonstick olive oil cooking
     spray
2   medium tomatoes, thinly
     sliced
4   ounces fresh mozzarella
     cheese, cut into 4 slices
½   cup fresh basil leaves
     Balsamic vinegar (optional)

1. Coat one side of each bread slice with cooking spray. Place bread slices on a work surface, coated sides down. Arrange tomatoes, mozzarella cheese, and basil on four of the bread slices. Cover with the remaining four bread slices, coated sides up; press together gently.

2. Preheat a covered indoor grill, panini press, grill pan, or large skillet. Place sandwiches, half at a time if necessary, in grill or panini press. Cover and cook for 3 to 4 minutes or until browned and cheese is melted. (If using a grill pan or skillet, place sandwiches on grill pan or skillet. Weight sandwiches with a heavy skillet [adding food cans for more weight] and cook for 2 to 3 minutes or until bread is toasted. Turn sandwiches, weight, and cook about 2 minutes more or until browned and cheese is melted.) If desired, serve with balsamic vinegar for dipping.

MAKES 4 SANDWICHES

Veggie Grilled Cheese

START TO FINISH: 20 minutes

NUTRITION FACTS
PER SANDWICH

Calories 359
Fat 14 g
Cholesterol 30 mg
Sodium 782 mg
Carbohydrates 42 g
Fiber 7 g
Protein 17 g

2 cups purchased pickled mixed vegetables (giardiniera)
3 cups packed fresh baby spinach
6 ounces fresh mozzarella cheese, chopped
½ cup oil-packed dried tomatoes, snipped
½ teaspoon ground black pepper
2 cloves garlic, minced, or 1 teaspoon bottled minced garlic
12 slices whole grain bread, toasted

1. Rinse and drain the pickled vegetables well. In a large microwave-safe bowl combine the pickled vegetables, spinach, cheese, tomatoes, pepper, and garlic.

2. Microwave on 100 percent power (high), uncovered, about 2 minutes or just until the mixture is warm, the spinach is wilted, and the cheese is beginning to melt.

3. To assemble sandwiches, layer half the cheese and vegetable mixture on four slices of toasted bread. Add another slice of bread and top with the remaining cheese and vegetable mixture and another slice of bread. Cut sandwiches diagonally into halves.
MAKES 4 SANDWICHES

Pita with Figs, Caramelized Onions, and Ricotta

START TO FINISH: 30 minutes

NUTRITION FACTS PER
OPEN-FACE SANDWICH

Calories 318
Fat 10 g
Cholesterol 17 mg
Sodium 383 mg
Carbohydrates 55 g
Fiber 5 g
Protein 8 g

1 tablespoon butter
1 tablespoon olive oil
1 large sweet onion, such
   as Vidalia or Maui, halved
   lengthwise and thinly sliced
1 teaspoon sugar
¼ teaspoon salt
⅛ teaspoon ground black pepper
1 tablespoon balsamic vinegar
½ cup part-skim ricotta cheese
1 tablespoon snipped fresh
   tarragon
2 whole wheat pita bread
   rounds
6 to 8 fresh figs, quartered
¼ cup chopped walnuts, toasted
   (see page 15) (optional)
¼ cup honey

1. For caramelized onions, in
a large skillet heat butter and
oil over medium-low heat. Add
onion. Cook, covered, for 13 to
15 minutes or until onion is tender,
stirring occasionally. Uncover; stir
in sugar, salt, and pepper. Cook
and stir over medium-high heat
for 3 to 5 minutes or until golden
brown. Add balsamic vinegar,
stirring to scrape up any browned
bits from the bottom of the skillet.
Remove from heat.

2. In a small bowl stir together
ricotta cheese and tarragon; set
aside.

3. Cut pita bread rounds in half
crosswise; wrap in microwave-
safe paper towels. Microwave on
100 percent power (high) for 10 to
20 seconds or just until warm.

4. Divide ricotta mixture among
pita halves, spreading evenly. Layer
with caramelized onions, figs,
and, if desired, walnuts. Drizzle
with honey. MAKES 4 OPEN-FACE
SANDWICHES

Make-Ahead Directions:
Prepare caramelized onions and
combine ricotta and tarragon.
Cover and chill up to 24 hours.
Reheat caramelized onions in a
microwave on 100 percent power
(high) for 1 minute.

Eggplant Parmesan Heros

PREP: 15 minutes
BAKE: 15 minutes
OVEN: 400°F

NUTRITION FACTS PER SANDWICH

Calories 423   *Fat* 9 g   *Cholesterol* 7 mg   *Sodium* 1,011 mg   *Carbohydrates* 73 g   *Fiber* 9 g   *Protein* 13 g

Nonstick cooking spray
1   medium eggplant (about
    1 pound)
1   cup seasoned croutons
⅓   cup shredded Parmesan
    cheese
1   cup purchased marinara
    sauce
4   bratwurst buns, split
    Fresh basil leaves (optional)

1. Preheat oven to 400°F. Lightly coat a baking sheet with cooking spray. Set aside. If desired, peel eggplant. Slice eggplant about ¼ inch thick.

2. Place croutons in a plastic bag. Use a rolling pin to crush croutons. In a shallow dish combine crushed croutons and ¼ cup of the cheese. Place marinara sauce in another shallow dish. Dip eggplant slices into marinara sauce and then into crushed croutons, pressing lightly to coat. Place on prepared baking sheet. Lightly coat eggplant with cooking spray.

3. Bake for 15 minutes or until coating is browned and eggplant is tender. Remove eggplant from oven. If desired, place buns, cut sides up, on a baking sheet; bake or broil buns for 2 minutes or until toasted.

4. Meanwhile, heat the remaining sauce in a small saucepan or in a small microwave-safe bowl in the microwave oven on high for 30 seconds.

5. Place eggplant slices on buns and top with remaining sauce and cheese. If desired, garnish with fresh basil. **MAKES 4 SANDWICHES**

Cheesy Eggplant Burgers

PREP: 15 minutes
GRILL: 6 minutes

NUTRITION FACTS PER BURGER

Calories 201
Fat 11 g
Cholesterol 17 mg
Sodium 506 mg
Carbohydrates 19 g
Fiber 4 g
Protein 3 g

1	teaspoon garlic powder
½	teaspoon ground black pepper
⅛	teaspoon salt
½	cup chopped, seeded tomato
2	tablespoons olive oil
1	tablespoon snipped fresh oregano
2	teaspoons snipped fresh thyme
2	teaspoons cider vinegar
6	½-inch slices eggplant
6	¾-ounce slices smoked Gouda cheese, cut in half
6	½-inch slices whole grain baguette-style bread, toasted

1. For seasoning, in a small bowl combine garlic powder, pepper, and salt. For tomato topping, in another small bowl combine half of the seasoning, chopped tomato, 1 tablespoon of the oil, the oregano, thyme, and vinegar. Set aside.

2. Brush eggplant slices with the remaining 1 tablespoon oil and sprinkle with the remaining seasoning.

3. For a charcoal or gas grill, place eggplant slices on the rack of an uncovered grill directly over medium heat. Cover and grill for 6 to 8 minutes or just until tender and golden brown, turning once halfway through grilling and topping with the cheese slices for the last 2 minutes of grilling.

4. Place eggplant slices on toasted bread. Spoon on tomato topping.
MAKES 6 BURGERS

Cumin-Crusted Veggie Burgers with Pineapple Salsa

START TO FINISH: 20 minutes

NUTRITION FACTS PER BURGER

Calories 316
Fat 5 g
Cholesterol 0 mg
Sodium 619 mg
Carbohydrates 52 g
Fiber 6 g
Protein 19 g

2   teaspoons cumin seeds
4   refrigerated or frozen
     meatless patties, thawed
     Olive oil
6   slices fresh or canned
     pineapple
4   pita bread rounds or
     flatbreads
1   tablespoon bottled pepper
     and onion relish
     Fresh basil leaves (optional)
     Chopped peanuts (optional)

1. In a medium skillet heat cumin seeds over medium heat for 3 to 4 minutes or until fragrant and starting to brown. Remove from skillet. Crush the seeds using a mortar and pestle or a rolling pin.

2. Brush patties with olive oil; coat with crushed cumin seeds. Blot excess moisture from pineapple slices and lightly coat with olive oil.

3. For a charcoal or gas grill, grill pineapple slices on the rack of a covered grill directly over medium-high heat for 6 to 8 minutes or until heated through, turning once halfway through grilling. Transfer

to a cutting board; set aside. Add patties to grill rack; grill about 8 minutes or until heated through, turning patties and adding pita bread after 4 minutes of grilling. Cover and keep warm.

4. For pineapple salsa, chop pineapple and place in a bowl. Stir in relish.

5. Serve veggie burgers on pita bread with pineapple salsa. If desired, top with fresh basil and chopped peanuts. **MAKES 4 BURGERS**

Spicy Seafood Tacos

START TO FINISH: 30 minutes

**NUTRITION FACTS
PER 2 TACOS**

Calories 302
Fat 12 g
Cholesterol 79 mg
Sodium 510 mg
Carbohydrates 28 g
Fiber 5 g
Protein 24 g

8   ounces fresh or frozen skinless red snapper fillets
8   ounces cooked lump crabmeat, cartilage removed
½   teaspoon dried oregano, crushed
½   teaspoon ground cumin
¼   teaspoon salt
⅛   to ¼ teaspoon cayenne pepper
3   cloves garlic, minced
    Nonstick cooking spray
½   cup light sour cream
1   teaspoon finely shredded lime peel
1½ cups finely shredded napa or savoy cabbage
1   medium mango, seeded, peeled, and chopped, or 1 cup chopped refrigerated mango slices
1   medium avocado, seeded, peeled, and chopped
6   tablespoons thinly sliced green onions (3)
½   to 1 medium fresh jalapeño chile pepper, thinly sliced (see tip, page 57)

1   tablespoon lime juice
1   teaspoon olive oil
⅛   teaspoon ground black pepper
8   6-inch corn tortillas, warmed according to package directions
¼   cup snipped fresh cilantro
    Lime wedges (optional)

1. Thaw fish, if frozen. Rinse fish; pat dry with paper towels. Cut fish into 1-inch pieces. Place fish and crabmeat in separate medium bowls. For spice mixture, in a small bowl combine oregano, cumin, ⅛ teaspoon of the salt, and the cayenne pepper. Add half the spice mixture and half the garlic to each bowl; toss gently to coat.

2. Coat a large nonstick skillet with cooking spray; heat skillet over medium heat. Add fish fillets; spread in an even layer. Cook, without stirring, for 2 minutes.

Add crabmeat. Cook for 2 to 3 minutes more or until fish flakes easily when tested with a fork and crabmeat is heated through, gently stirring occasionally.

3. For dressing, in a small bowl combine sour cream and lime peel; set aside.

4. In a medium bowl combine cabbage, mango, avocado, green onions, and jalapeño pepper. For dressing, in a small bowl combine lime juice, oil, black pepper, and the remaining ⅛ teaspoon salt. Pour dressing over cabbage mixture; toss gently to coat.

5. To assemble, spoon fish mixture onto each warm tortilla. Top with cabbage mixture and cilantro. Fold tortilla over filling. Serve with dressing and, if desired, lime wedges.
MAKES 8 TACOS

CHAPTER 4

Main-Dish Salads

Wilted Chicken Salad with Pomegranate Dressing

START TO FINISH: 30 minutes

NUTRITION FACTS PER SERVING

Calories 292
Fat 11 g
Cholesterol 58 mg
Sodium 425 mg
Carbohydrates 21 g
Fiber 4 g
Protein 27 g

¾ cup pomegranate juice

2 tablespoons olive oil

1 14- to 16-ounce package chicken tenderloins

½ medium red onion, cut lengthwise into thin wedges

1 tablespoon snipped fresh oregano or ½ teaspoon dried oregano, crushed

¾ teaspoon coarsely ground black pepper

½ teaspoon salt

2 tablespoons red wine vinegar

2 6-ounce packages fresh baby spinach

½ cup pomegranate seeds

¼ cup slivered almonds, toasted (see tip, page 15)

1. In a small saucepan bring pomegranate juice to boiling; boil gently, uncovered, for 5 to 8 minutes or until reduced to ¼ cup. Remove from heat; set aside. Meanwhile, in an extra-large skillet heat 1 tablespoon of the oil over medium-high heat. Add chicken and cook for 6 to 8 minutes or until chicken is tender and no longer pink (170°F), turning occasionally. Remove chicken from skillet. Keep warm.

2. Add the remaining 1 tablespoon oil, the onion, dried oregano (if using), pepper, and salt to skillet; cook for 3 to 5 minutes or just until onion is tender, stirring occasionally. Stir in reduced pomegranate juice and the vinegar; bring to boiling. Boil 1 minute.

Remove skillet from heat. Stir in fresh oregano (if using). Gradually add spinach, tossing just until spinach is wilted.

3. Transfer spinach mixture to a large shallow dish. Top with chicken, pomegranate seeds, and almonds. Serve immediately.

MAKES 4 SERVINGS

Buffalo Chicken Salad

START TO FINISH: 15 minutes

NUTRITION FACTS
PER SERVING

Calories 297
Fat 10 g
Cholesterol 99 mg
Sodium 596 mg
Carbohydrates 13 g
Fiber 3 g
Protein 37 g

2   hearts of romaine, sliced
3   cups coarsely chopped cooked
     chicken breast
½   cup Buffalo wing sauce
4   21-gram wedges light blue
     cheese, crumbled
1   teaspoon cracked black
     pepper
¼   cup bottled fat-free blue
     cheese salad dressing
4   teaspoons fat-free milk
4   stalks celery, each cut into
     4 sticks

1. Divide romaine among four
serving plates or bowls.

2. In a medium microwave-safe
bowl combine chicken and wing
sauce. Microwave on 100 percent
power (high) about 60 seconds
or until heated through. Evenly
divide chicken mixture and spoon
over romaine. Top with crumbled
cheese and pepper.

3. In a small bowl combine salad
dressing and milk; drizzle over
salads. Serve with celery sticks.
MAKES 4 SERVINGS

BBQ Chicken and Roasted Corn Salad

PREP: 25 minutes
BROIL: 6 minutes

NUTRITION FACTS PER SERVING

Calories 345   *Fat* 11 g   *Cholesterol* 80 mg   *Sodium* 435 mg   *Carbohydrates* 30 g   *Fiber* 8 g   *Protein* 33 g

1   to 1¼ pounds skinless, boneless chicken breast halves
2   teaspoons ground ancho chile pepper or chili powder
1   teaspoon dried oregano, crushed
1   teaspoon dried thyme, crushed
¼   teaspoon salt
¼   teaspoon ground black pepper
1   15-ounce can no-salt-added black beans, rinsed and drained
1   cup frozen whole kernel corn, thawed
1   tablespoon canola oil
2   tablespoons light ranch salad dressing
2   tablespoons low-sodium barbecue sauce
1   tablespoon white wine vinegar
4   cups chopped romaine lettuce
1   cup cherry tomatoes, halved
1   ounce queso fresco, crumbled, or Monterey Jack cheese, shredded (¼ cup)

1. Place each chicken breast half between two pieces of plastic wrap. Using the flat side of a meat mallet, pound the chicken to about ½-inch thickness. Remove the plastic wrap.

2. Preheat broiler. In a small bowl stir together ground chile pepper, oregano, thyme, salt, and black pepper. Sprinkle half the spice mixture evenly over chicken pieces; rub in with your fingers.

3. In a medium bowl combine beans, corn, oil, and the remaining spice mixture. Stir to combine.

4. Line a 15×10×1-inch baking pan with foil. Place chicken on one side of the pan. Add bean mixture to the opposite side. Broil 4 to 5 inches from the heat for 6 to 8 minutes or until chicken is tender and no longer pink (170°F), turning chicken and stirring the bean mixture once halfway through broiling.

5. Meanwhile, in a small bowl combine salad dressing, barbecue sauce, and vinegar; set aside.

6. To assemble, divide romaine among four serving plates. Slice chicken. Top romaine with bean mixture, chicken, and tomatoes, dividing evenly. Sprinkle with queso fresco and serve with salad dressing mixture. **MAKES 4 SERVINGS**

Mango Chicken Salad

START TO FINISH: 30 minutes
OVEN: 350°F

NUTRITION FACTS PER SERVING

Calories 302
Fat 10 g
Cholesterol 62 mg
Sodium 381 mg
Carbohydrates 29 g
Fiber 4 g
Protein 27 g

3   skinless, boneless chicken breast halves (12 to 16 ounces total)
2   limes
1   cup unsweetened coconut milk
1   tablespoon soy sauce
½   teaspoon crushed red pepper
½   cup flaked unsweetened coconut
2   mangoes, seeded, peeled, and chopped
    Lettuce leaves (optional)

1. Preheat oven to 350°F. Cut chicken into bite-size pieces. Squeeze juice from 1 lime; set juice aside. Cut the remaining lime into wedges; set aside.

2. In a large saucepan stir together the lime juice, the coconut milk, soy sauce, and crushed red pepper. Add chicken. Bring to boiling; reduce heat. Cook, covered, for 12 to 15 minutes or until chicken is tender and no longer pink, stirring occasionally.

3. Meanwhile, spread coconut in a shallow baking pan. Bake, uncovered, for 4 to 5 minutes or until golden, stirring once.

4. Transfer chicken and cooking liquid to a large bowl. Add mangoes; toss to coat. Arrange lettuce leaves on serving plates; top with chicken mixture. Sprinkle with toasted coconut and serve with lime wedges. **MAKES 4 SERVINGS**

Pulled Chicken-Peanut Salad

START TO FINISH: 25 minutes

NUTRITION FACTS PER SERVING

Calories 263
Fat 12 g
Cholesterol 62 mg
Sodium 247 mg
Carbohydrates 15 g
Fiber 2 g
Protein 24 g

2 tablespoons frozen orange juice concentrate, thawed
1 tablespoon water
2 teaspoons toasted sesame oil
¼ teaspoon salt
⅛ teaspoon coarsely ground black pepper
6 cups torn mixed salad greens
2 cups coarsely shredded cooked chicken (10 ounces)
1 11-ounce can mandarin orange sections, drained
¼ cup cocktail peanuts

1. For dressing, in a small bowl stir together juice concentrate, water, sesame oil, salt, and pepper. Set aside.

2. Arrange greens on salad plates. Top with chicken, oranges, and peanuts. Drizzle with dressing.
MAKES 4 SERVINGS

Smoked Turkey and Bacon Salad

START TO FINISH: 20 minutes

NUTRITION FACTS PER SERVING

Calories 258   *Fat* 14 g   *Cholesterol* 68 mg   *Sodium* 601 mg   *Carbohydrates* 9 g   *Fiber* 3 g   *Protein* 23 g

5   slices low-sodium bacon
2   cups sugar snap peas
½   cup light mayonnaise
1   tablespoon Dijon mustard
1   tablespoon cider vinegar
1   tablespoon snipped fresh dill
1   small head romaine, torn
8   ounces smoked turkey breast, cut into bite-size strips

1. Line a 9-inch microwave-safe pie plate with paper towels. Arrange bacon slices in a single layer on paper towels. Cover with additional paper towels. Microwave on 100 percent power (high) for 4 to 5 minutes or until bacon is crisp. Carefully remove the pie plate from the microwave. Set cooked bacon slices aside to cool.

2. Meanwhile, in a medium-size covered saucepan cook the sugar snap peas in a small amount of boiling salted water for 2 to 4 minutes or until crisp-tender; drain. Crumble one bacon slice; set aside. Break remaining bacon slices into 1-inch pieces.

3. For dressing, in a small bowl combine mayonnaise, mustard, vinegar, and dill. Stir in crumbled bacon.

4. Divide romaine among four plates. Top with sugar snap peas, turkey, and bacon pieces. Serve with dressing. **MAKES 4 SERVINGS**

Turkey Salad with Oranges

START TO FINISH: 30 minutes

NUTRITION FACTS
PER SERVING

Calories 281
Fat 8 g fats
Cholesterol 71 mg
Sodium 263 mg
Carbohydrates 25 g
Fiber 5 g
Protein 28 g

1   5-ounce package arugula or
    baby spinach
2½ cups shredded cooked turkey
    or chicken (12 ounces)
1   large red sweet pepper, cut
    into strips (1 cup)
¼   cup snipped fresh cilantro
3   tablespoons orange juice
2   tablespoons peanut oil or
    canola oil
1   tablespoon honey
2   teaspoons lemon juice
2   teaspoons Dijon mustard
¼   teaspoon ground cumin
¼   teaspoon salt
¼   teaspoon ground black pepper
4   oranges, peeled and sectioned

1. In a large bowl toss together arugula, turkey, sweet pepper, and cilantro. Set aside.

2. For vinaigrette, in a small bowl whisk together orange juice, oil, honey, lemon juice, mustard, cumin, salt, and black pepper. Drizzle vinaigrette over salad; toss gently to coat. Add orange sections to salad. **MAKES 4 SERVINGS**

Pork and Apple Salad with Blue Cheese Dressing

PREP: 20 minutes
BROIL: 6 minutes

NUTRITION FACTS PER SERVING

Calories 234
Fat 11 g
Cholesterol 61 mg
Sodium 203 mg
Carbohydrates 14 g
Fiber 3 g
Protein 21 g

⅓ cup buttermilk
2 tablespoons light mayonnaise
2 tablespoons crumbled blue cheese
2 tablespoons thinly sliced green onion (1)
12 ounces boneless pork top loin chops, cut ¾ inch thick
2 teaspoons snipped fresh thyme or 1 teaspoon dried thyme, crushed
¼ teaspoon ground black pepper
8 cups torn mixed salad greens
2 cups thinly sliced apples and/or pears (2 medium)
¼ cup coarsely chopped walnuts, toasted (see tip, page 15) (optional)
    Cracked black pepper (optional)

1. Preheat broiler. For dressing, in a small bowl whisk together buttermilk and mayonnaise until smooth. Stir in cheese and green onion. Set aside.

2. Trim fat from chops. Sprinkle thyme and the ground black pepper evenly over both sides of chops; rub in with your fingers. Place chops on the unheated rack of a broiler pan. Broil 3 to 4 inches from the heat for 6 to 8 minutes or until done (145°F), turning once halfway through broiling time.

3. Divide salad greens and apples among dinner plates. Slice chops; arrange on top of greens and apples. Drizzle with dressing. If desired, sprinkle with walnuts and cracked pepper. **MAKES 4 SERVINGS**

Escarole and Poached Egg Salad

START TO FINISH: 20 minutes

NUTRITION FACTS PER SERVING

Calories 272   *Fat* 13 g   *Cholesterol* 215 mg   *Sodium* 432 mg   *Carbohydrates* 23 g   *Fiber* 8 g   *Protein* 17 g

8   cups torn escarole or arugula
1   large tomato, halved
½   cup frozen peas, thawed
4   eggs
1   recipe Red Wine Vinaigrette
¼   cup finely shredded Parmesan cheese (1 ounce)
4   slices whole grain country-style bread, toasted

1. On a serving platter combine escarole, tomato, and peas; set aside.

2. In a large deep skillet add enough water to fill halfway. Bring water to a simmer. Break eggs, one at a time, into a small cup and slide into water.* Cook eggs in simmering water for 4 to 5 minutes or until whites are firm and yolks begin to thicken. Remove eggs with slotted spoon; drain on paper towels.

3. Place eggs on salad. Drizzle with Red Wine Vinaigrette. Sprinkle with Parmesan cheese. Serve with toast. **MAKES 4 SERVINGS**

Red Wine Vinaigrette: In a screw-top jar combine 2 tablespoons red wine vinegar; 4 teaspoons olive oil; 1 teaspoon snipped fresh oregano or ½ teaspoon dried oregano, crushed; ½ teaspoon Dijon mustard; ¼ teaspoon cracked black pepper; and ⅛ teaspoon salt. Cover and shake well to combine.

*Tip: To keep poached eggs intact, add a teaspoon or so of vinegar to the boiling water, then slip in the eggs. Vinegar helps the egg whites keep their shape by quickly firming up and congealing the edges.

Teriyaki Shrimp and Edamame Salad

START TO FINISH: 25 minutes

NUTRITION FACTS PER SERVING

Calories 181
Fat 7 g
Cholesterol 90 mg
Sodium 593 mg
Carbohydrates 15 g
Fiber 4 g
Protein 15 g

½ cup frozen sweet soybeans (edamame)
2 ounces dried radiatore or rotini pasta
3 cups packaged fresh baby spinach
2 cups shredded romaine lettuce
¾ cup coarsely shredded carrots
¾ cup fresh pea pods, trimmed, strings removed, and halved
1 small red or yellow sweet pepper, cut into thin strips
¼ cup thinly sliced green onions
6 ounces cooked medium shrimp, halved horizontally
3 tablespoons rice vinegar or cider vinegar
1 tablespoon canola oil
1 tablespoon reduced-sodium soy sauce
4 cloves garlic, minced
1 teaspoon toasted sesame oil
1 teaspoon grated fresh ginger
⅛ teaspoon crushed red pepper

1. Cook soybeans according to package directions; drain. Cook pasta according to package directions; drain and rinse with cold water.

2. Arrange spinach and romaine on a large serving platter. Top with carrots, pea pods, sweet pepper, sweet soybeans, and green onions. In a medium bowl combine shrimp and cooked pasta; set aside.

3. For dressing, in a screw-top jar combine vinegar, canola oil, soy sauce, garlic, toasted sesame oil, ginger, and crushed red pepper. Cover and shake well to combine. Pour half the dressing over the shrimp and pasta; toss to coat.

4. Top salad on serving platter with shrimp and pasta. Drizzle salad with remaining salad dressing. **MAKES 4 SERVINGS**

Ginger Shrimp and Soba Salad

PREP: 25 minutes
MARINATE: 1 hour
COOK: 10 minutes

NUTRITION FACTS PER SERVING

Calories 356
Fat 6 g
Cholesterol 172 mg
Sodium 336 mg
Carbohydrates 42 g
Fiber 2 g
Protein 29 g

1   pound fresh or frozen large shrimp
⅓   cup rice vinegar
2   tablespoons finely chopped onion
1   tablespoon grated fresh ginger
1   tablespoon reduced-sodium soy sauce
6   ounces dried soba (buckwheat) noodles, vermicelli noodles, or udon noodles
    Nonstick cooking spray
1   tablespoon canola oil
1½ cups fresh baby spinach leaves or torn romaine
1   recipe Gingered Tropical Fruit Salsa

1. Thaw shrimp, if frozen. Peel and devein shrimp, leaving tails intact if desired. Rinse shrimp; pat dry with paper towels. Set aside.

2. For vinaigrette, in a screw-top jar combine rice vinegar, onion, ginger, and soy sauce; cover and shake well. Reserve ¼ cup of the vinaigrette; cover and chill.

3. Place shrimp in a resealable plastic bag set in a shallow dish. Pour remaining vinaigrette over shrimp. Seal bag; turn to coat shrimp. Marinate in the refrigerator for 1 to 2 hours, turning bag occasionally.

4. Cook soba according to package directions; drain. Keep warm.

5. Meanwhile, drain shrimp, discarding marinade. Lightly coat a large unheated skillet with cooking spray. Preheat over medium-high heat. Add shrimp to skillet; cook and stir for 1 to 3 minutes or just until shrimp are just opaque.

6. In a large bowl combine the reserved ¼ cup vinaigrette and the canola oil; whisk until combined. Add warm soba, shrimp, spinach, and 1 cup of the Gingered Tropical Fruit Salsa; toss gently to coat. Serve immediately.

MAKES 4 SERVINGS

Gingered Tropical Fruit Salsa: In a medium bowl combine 1 tablespoon snipped fresh mint, 2 teaspoons seasoned rice vinegar, 2 teaspoons lime juice, ½ to 1 teaspoon grated fresh ginger, and ⅛ teaspoon crushed red pepper. Add ½ cup chopped fresh pineapple; ½ cup chopped mango or peach; 2 kiwifruits, peeled, quartered lengthwise, and sliced; and one 5-ounce container mandarin orange sections. Toss gently. Makes 2 cups.

Bulgur-Mango Salad

PREP: 20 minutes
STAND: 1 hour

NUTRITION FACTS PER SERVING

Calories 274
Fat 12 g
Cholesterol 20 mg
Sodium 544 mg
Carbohydrates 36 g
Fiber 8 g
Protein 10 g

½   cup bulgur
3   cups boiling water
1   15-ounce can reduced-sodium garbanzo beans (chickpeas), rinsed and drained
1½ cups chopped fresh or frozen mango
½   cup chopped red onion (1 medium)
⅓   cup lime juice
2   tablespoons canola oil
½   teaspoon ground cinnamon
¼   teaspoon salt
¼   teaspoon ground cumin
⅛   teaspoon cayenne pepper
3   tablespoons snipped fresh mint
5   cups mixed spring salad greens
4   ounces feta cheese, crumbled
     Snipped fresh mint (optional)

1. Pour boiling water over bulgur; cover with plastic wrap. Let stand at room temperature 1 hour.

2. Meanwhile, in a large bowl stir together garbanzo beans, mango, and onion. Set aside. For dressing, in a small bowl whisk together lime juice, canola oil, cinnamon, salt, cumin, and cayenne pepper.

3. Drain any water off bulgur. Add bulgur, dressing, and the 3 tablespoons mint to the bean mixture, stirring to mix well. Evenly divide salad greens among five serving plates. Top each with 1 cup of the bulgur-bean mixture. Sprinkle with feta cheese. If desired, garnish with additional fresh mint. **MAKES 5 SERVINGS**

Soy-Glazed Flank Steak with Blistered Green Beans

START TO FINISH: 30 minutes

NUTRITION FACTS PER SERVING

Calories 312
Fat 16 g
Cholesterol 53 mg
Sodium 672 mg
Carbohydrates 15 g
Fiber 4 g
Protein 28 g

1   pound fresh green beans
1   pound beef flank steak
6   cloves garlic, minced
1   tablespoon grated fresh ginger
2   tablespoons soy sauce
1   teaspoon packed brown sugar
2   to 3 tablespoons peanut oil
4   green onions, white parts only, thinly sliced
2   tablespoons sweet rice wine (mirin)
1   teaspoon red chile paste (sambal oelek)
    Sesame seeds, toasted* (optional)
    Hot cooked jasmine rice (optional)

1. Trim green beans; set aside. Trim fat from beef. Thinly slice meat across the grain into narrow strips. Set beef aside. In a small bowl combine garlic and ginger; set aside. In another small bowl combine soy sauce and brown sugar; set aside.

2. In a wok or extra-large skillet heat 2 tablespoons of the oil over medium-high heat. Add green beans; cook and stir for 7 to 8 minutes or until beans are blistered and brown in spots. Transfer beans to paper towels to drain. If necessary, add the remaining 1 tablespoon oil to wok.

3. Add garlic and ginger to the wok; cook and stir for 30 seconds. Add half the beef strips to the wok. Cook and stir about 3 minutes or until meat is slightly pink in the center. Using a slotted spoon, transfer meat to a medium bowl. Cook the remaining beef. Return all beef to skillet. Stir in green onions, rice wine, chile paste, and the soy sauce mixture. Cook and stir for 1 minute; add green beans. Cook and stir about 2 minutes to heat through.

4. If desired, sprinkle with sesame seeds and serve with hot cooked rice. **MAKES 4 SERVINGS**

*Tip:** To toast sesame seeds, scatter them in a small dry skillet. Heat over medium heat just until golden. Stir frequently to prevent seeds from burning.

Herbed Steaks with Horseradish

START TO FINISH: 20 minutes

NUTRITION FACTS
PER SERVING

Calories 284
Fat 15 g
Cholesterol 84 mg
Sodium 351 mg
Carbohydrates 1 g
Fiber 0 g
Protein 33 g

2   12- to 14-ounce beef top loin
    steaks, cut 1 inch thick
    Salt
    Ground black pepper
2   tablespoons prepared
    horseradish
1   tablespoon Dijon mustard
2   teaspoons snipped fresh
    Italian (flat-leaf) parsley
1   teaspoon snipped fresh thyme
    Broiled cherry tomatoes
    (optional)
    Broiled sweet pepper strips
    (optional)
    Herbed mayonnaise
    (optional)

1. Preheat broiler. Trim fat from steaks. Lightly sprinkle steaks with salt and pepper. Place steaks on the unheated rack of a broiler pan. Broil 4 to 5 inches from heat for 7 minutes.

2. Meanwhile, for horseradish sauce, in a small bowl stir together horseradish, mustard, parsley, and thyme.

3. Turn steaks. Broil for 8 to 9 minutes more for medium (160°F). The last 1 minute of broiling, spread horseradish sauce over steaks. If desired, serve with tomatoes, peppers, and herbed mayonnaise. **MAKES 4 SERVINGS**

Five-Spice Beef Kabobs

START TO FINISH: **20 minutes**

NUTRITION FACTS PER SERVING

Calories 213   *Fat* 8 g   *Cholesterol* 74 mg   *Sodium* 366 mg   *Carbohydrates* 5 g   *Fiber* 1 g   *Protein* 29 g

1   pound beef flank steak or boneless beef sirloin
2   tablespoons reduced-sodium soy sauce
1   to 1½ teaspoons Chinese five-spice powder
1   6-ounce carton plain Greek yogurt
1   tablespoon snipped fresh mint leaves
2   small limes
    Fresh mint leaves

1. Trim fat from beef. Thinly slice beef across the grain. If necessary, flatten slices with palm of hand or meat mallet to ¼-inch thickness. In a medium bowl combine beef, soy sauce, and five-spice powder; toss to coat beef. Thread beef on skewers.*

2. For a charcoal or gas grill, grill kabobs on the rack of a covered grill directly over medium heat for 4 to 6 minutes or to desired doneness, turning once.

3. Meanwhile, in a small bowl combine yogurt and 1 tablespoon snipped mint. From one lime, finely shred 1 teaspoon peel. Juice the lime. Stir peel and 1 tablespoon juice into yogurt. Cut remaining lime in wedges. Serve kabobs with yogurt sauce, mint leaves, and lime wedges. **MAKES 4 SERVINGS**

*Tip: If using wooden skewers, soak in enough water to cover for at least 30 minutes before using.

Tip: To serve with fresh carrot ribbons, use a vegetable peeler to cut thin ribbons from whole long carrots. Toss with a squeeze of lime juice and lightly sprinkle with five-spice powder.

Barbecued Beef Kabobs: Prepare as directed, except substitute bottled barbecue sauce for the soy sauce, chili powder for the Chinese-five spice powder, sour cream for the yogurt, and cilantro for mint.

Frizzled Eggs over Garlic Steak and Mushroom Hash

START TO FINISH: 30 minutes

NUTRITION FACTS PER SERVING

Calories 351
Fat 16 g
Cholesterol 233 mg
Sodium 295 mg
Carbohydrates 22 g
Fiber 1 g
Protein 30 g

2   tablespoons vegetable oil
2   cups frozen diced hash brown potatoes with onions and peppers
1   8-ounce package sliced fresh mushrooms
4   3- to 4-ounce thin breakfast steaks
    Salt
    Ground black pepper
4   to 6 cloves garlic, thinly sliced
4   eggs
    Fresh tarragon (optional)

1. In an extra-large skillet heat 1 tablespoon of the oil. Cook potatoes and mushrooms, covered, over medium-high heat for 10 minutes. Stir occasionally. Remove from skillet; cover to keep warm.

2. Sprinkle steaks with salt and pepper. Heat remaining 1 tablespoon oil in skillet. Cook steaks and garlic for 3 to 4 minutes, turning once, until desired doneness. Remove from skillet; cover to keep warm.

3. Add eggs to the hot skillet; sprinkle with salt and pepper. Cook to desired doneness. Place potatoes, steaks, and eggs on plates. If desired, sprinkle with fresh tarragon. **MAKES 4 SERVINGS**

Serving Suggestion: If you like, top the hash with sour cream, a bit of jarred horseradish, and a pinch of fresh snipped herbs.

Grilled Steaks with Roasted Garlic

PREP: 20 minutes
GRILL: 30 minutes

1   whole bulb garlic
3   to 4 teaspoons snipped fresh basil or 1 teaspoon dried basil, crushed
1   tablespoon snipped fresh rosemary or 1 teaspoon dried rosemary, crushed
2   tablespoons olive oil or vegetable oil
1½ pounds boneless beef ribeye steaks or sirloin steak, cut 1 inch thick
1   to 2 teaspoons cracked black pepper
½   teaspoon salt

1. Cut off the top ½ inch of the garlic bulb to expose the tips of individual cloves. Leaving garlic bulb whole, remove any loose papery outer layers.

2. Fold a 20×18-inch piece of heavy foil in half crosswise; trim to a double-thick 10-inch square. Place garlic bulb, cut side up, in the center of foil. Sprinkle with basil and rosemary; drizzle with oil. Bring up two opposite edges of foil; seal with a double fold. Fold the remaining ends to completely enclose garlic, leaving space for steam to build.

3. For a charcoal or gas grill, grill garlic in foil packet on the rack of a covered grill directly over medium heat about 30 minutes or until garlic feels soft when packet is squeezed, turning occasionally during grilling.

4. Meanwhile, trim fat from steaks. Evenly sprinkle pepper and salt on both sides of each steak; rub in with your fingers. While garlic grills, add steaks to grill. Cover and grill until steaks reach desired doneness, turning once halfway through grilling time. For ribeye steaks, allow 10 to 12 minutes for medium rare (145°F) or 12 to 15 minutes for medium (160°F). For sirloin steak, allow 14 to 18 minutes for medium rare (145°F) or 18 to 22 minutes for medium (160°F).

5. Remove garlic from foil, reserving herb mixture. Squeeze garlic pulp onto steaks. Mash pulp slightly to spread it over steaks. To serve, cut steaks into six serving-size pieces. Drizzle steaks with reserved herb mixture.
MAKES 6 SERVINGS

Garlic-Lime Skirt Steak with Jalapeños and Grilled Tomato-Pepper Chutney

PREP: 20 minutes   MARINATE: 2 hours
STAND: 30 minutes   GRILL: 15 minutes

NUTRITION FACTS PER SERVING

Calories 245   *Fat* 11 g   *Cholesterol* 74 mg   *Sodium* 473 mg   *Carbohydrates* 10 g   *Fiber* 2 g   *Protein* 25 g

2   pounds beef skirt or flank steak, cut ½ to ¾ inch thick
2   tablespoons lime juice
2   tablespoons balsamic vinegar
2   tablespoons minced garlic (12 cloves)
1   tablespoon vegetable oil
1   teaspoon kosher salt
½   teaspoon ground black pepper
⅓   cup finely snipped fresh cilantro
8   to 10 miniature sweet peppers
1   recipe Grilled Tomato-Yellow Pepper Chutney

1. Trim fat from steak. Place steak in a large resealable plastic bag set in a shallow dish. In a small bowl whisk together lime juice, vinegar, garlic, oil, salt, and black pepper. Stir in cilantro. Pour over steak in bag; seal bag. Turn to coat. Marinate in the refrigerator 2 to 24 hours, turning bag occasionally. Drain steak, discarding marinade. Allow steak to stand at room temperature 30 minutes.

2. For a charcoal or gas grill, grill steak on the rack of a covered grill directly over medium-high heat 10 to 12 minutes or until internal temperature reaches 145°F for medium rare, turning once halfway through grilling time. Let steak stand 5 minutes; thinly slice.

3. While steak stands, grill the sweet peppers on the grill rack directly over medium heat about 5 minutes or until lightly charred, turning frequently. Serve sliced steak with grilled peppers and Grilled Tomato-Yellow Pepper Chutney. **MAKES 8 SERVINGS**

Grilled Tomato-Yellow Pepper Chutney: For a charcoal or gas grill, grill 1 large yellow sweet pepper on the rack of a covered grill directly over medium heat about 20 minutes or until skin is charred and pepper is tender, turning often to evenly char the skin. Remove from grill and wrap in foil. Let stand about 15 minutes or until cool enough to handle. Using a sharp knife, loosen the edges of the skin from the pepper. Gently and slowly pull off the skin in strips. Chop pepper; set aside. Seed and chop 2 medium tomatoes. In a 9-inch round disposable foil pan combine tomatoes, ½ cup chopped onion, ½ teaspoon salt, and ¼ to ½ teaspoon crushed red pepper. Cover tightly with foil. Place pan on the grill rack directly over medium heat; cover and grill 20 minutes. Remove foil. Stir in the chopped sweet pepper, 2 tablespoons snipped fresh cilantro, and 1 tablespoon honey. Grill, uncovered, about 5 minutes more or until most of the liquid has evaporated. Transfer to a serving bowl. Cool about 30 minutes or until chutney is at room temperature before serving.

Sirloin Steak with Deep Red Wine Reduction

PREP: 15 minutes
MARINATE: 8 hours
COOK: 10 minutes
STAND: 3 minutes

NUTRITION FACTS PER SERVING

Calories 162
Fat 5 g
Cholesterol 61 mg
Sodium 297 mg
Carbohydrates 4 g
Fiber 0 g
Protein 20 g

½ cup dry red wine
2 tablespoons balsamic vinegar
1 tablespoon reduced-sodium soy sauce
2 teaspoons instant coffee granules
2 teaspoons Worcestershire sauce
½ teaspoon coarsely ground black pepper
1 pound boneless beef sirloin steak, trimmed and cut about ¾ inch thick
⅛ teaspoon salt
Nonstick cooking spray
Steamed sliced zucchini and/or yellow summer squash (optional)
Snipped fresh oregano (optional)

1. For marinade, in a small bowl combine wine, vinegar, soy sauce, coffee granules, Worcestershire sauce, and pepper. Place the steak in a large resealable plastic bag set in a shallow dish. Pour ¼ cup marinade on the steak. Seal bag; turn to coat steak. Marinate in the refrigerator 8 to 24 hours, turning occasionally. Stir the salt into the remaining marinade; cover and chill until needed.

2. Lightly coat a grill pan with cooking spray. Heat over medium-high heat. Drain steak, discarding marinade. Cook steak on hot grill pan 10 to 12 minutes or until desired doneness (145°F for medium rare), turning once halfway through cooking time. Transfer steak to a cutting board. Let stand 3 minutes; thinly slice steak.

3. Meanwhile, for wine reduction, in a small saucepan heat the reserved marinade to boiling over medium-high heat. Boil, uncovered, 2 to 3 minutes or until reduced to ¼ cup. (For a more concentrated sauce, reduce to 2 tablespoons.) Spoon wine reduction over sliced steak. If desired, serve with zucchini and/or sprinkle with oregano.
MAKES 4 SERVINGS

Beef Medallions with Horseradish Sauce and Mashed Vegetables

PREP: 35 minutes
COOK: 26 minutes

NUTRITION FACTS PER SERVING

Calories 243
Fat 11 g
Cholesterol 81 mg
Sodium 189 mg
Carbohydrates 2 g
Fiber 9 g
Protein 32 g

1   recipe Mashed Vegetables
20 ounces boneless beef shoulder tenders
½   teaspoon lemon-pepper seasoning or freshly ground black pepper
2   teaspoons olive oil
½   cup plain fat-free Greek yogurt
2   tablespoons prepared horseradish
⅛   teaspoon salt

1. Prepare Mashed Vegetables. Meanwhile, cut beef crosswise into 1-inch slices. Place each slice between two pieces of plastic wrap. Using the flat side of a meat mallet, lightly pound beef to ¼-inch thickness. Discard plastic wrap. Sprinkle beef with lemon-pepper seasoning.

2. In an extra-large skillet heat oil over medium-high heat. Cook beef in hot oil for 4 to 6 minutes or until medium, turning once halfway through cooking.

3. For horseradish sauce, stir together the yogurt, horseradish, and ⅛ teaspoon salt. Serve beef and mashed vegetables with horseradish sauce. **MAKES 4 SERVINGS**

Mashed Vegetables: In a Dutch oven combine 3 cups peeled and cut-up turnips; 2 cups peeled and cut-up carrots; 2 cups peeled and cut-up parsnips; and 1 medium onion, cut into wedges. Add enough water to cover. Bring to boiling; reduce heat. Cover and simmer for 25 to 30 minutes or until vegetables are tender. Drain well. Return vegetables to hot pan. Mash vegetables with potato masher while adding 2 tablespoons butter, 2 tablespoons fat-free milk, ½ teaspoon salt, and ⅛ teaspoon ground black pepper. Vegetables should still have plenty of texture and not be completely smooth.

Roast Beef with Mushroom-Fig Sauce

PREP: 20 minutes **ROAST:** 1 hour 30 minutes
STAND: 15 minutes **COOK:** 18 minutes **OVEN:** 325°F

NUTRITION FACTS PER SERVING

Calories 243 *Fat* 10 g *Cholesterol* 46 mg *Sodium* 226 mg *Carbohydrates* 8 g *Fiber* 1 g *Protein* 26 g

1 2- to 2½-pound beef eye round roast
½ teaspoon cracked black pepper
¼ teaspoon salt
1 tablespoon olive oil
8 ounces fresh cremini, stemmed shiitake, or button mushrooms, sliced
2 tablespoons finely chopped shallot or sweet onion
½ cup dry red wine or lower-sodium beef broth
1 tablespoon Dijon mustard
1 teaspoon snipped fresh rosemary or ½ teaspoon dried rosemary, crushed
¾ cup lower-sodium beef broth
½ cup chopped, stemmed dried figs
   Fresh rosemary sprigs

1. Preheat oven to 325°F. Trim fat from meat. Sprinkle meat with the pepper and salt; rub in with your fingers.

2. Place meat on a rack in a shallow roasting pan. Insert an oven-going meat thermometer into center of roast. Roast, uncovered, for 1½ to 1¾ hours or until thermometer registers 135°F (it is not recommended to roast an eye round roast past medium rare). Cover meat with foil; let stand for 15 minutes before slicing. Meat temperature after standing should be 145°F.

3. Meanwhile for mushroom-fig sauce, in a large skillet heat oil over medium heat. Add mushrooms and shallot to skillet. Cook over medium heat for 5 to 8 minutes or just until mushrooms are tender and lightly browned, stirring occasionally. Remove from heat and add wine to skillet. Return to heat and bring to boiling; boil gently, uncovered, about 3 minutes or until wine is reduced by about half. Whisk in mustard and the 1 teaspoon rosemary. Add broth and figs. Bring to boiling; boil gently, uncovered, about 10 minutes or until liquid is slightly thickened and reduced by about one-third.

4. Thinly slice meat and serve with mushroom-fig sauce. Garnish with rosemary sprigs. **MAKES 8 SERVINGS**

Slow-Cooked Beef with Carrots and Cabbage

PREP: 20 minutes
SLOW COOK: 7 hours (low) or 3½ hours (high) + 30 minutes (high)

NUTRITION FACTS PER SERVING

Calories 214
Fat 5 g
Cholesterol 50 mg
Sodium 379 mg
Carbohydrates 14 g
Fiber 5 g
Protein 27 g

8   ounces boneless beef chuck pot roast
¼   teaspoon dried oregano, crushed
¼   teaspoon ground cumin
¼   teaspoon paprika
¼   teaspoon ground black pepper
⅛   teaspoon salt
    Nonstick cooking spray
3   medium carrots, cut into 2-inch pieces
2   small cloves garlic, minced
⅓   cup lower-sodium beef broth
2   cups coarsely shredded cabbage

1. Trim fat from roast. In a small bowl combine oregano, cumin, paprika, pepper, and salt. Evenly sprinkle mixture over meat; rub in with your fingers. Coat a medium nonstick skillet with cooking spray; heat skillet over medium heat. Add meat to skillet; brown on all sides.

2. Meanwhile, in a 1½- or 2-quart slow cooker combine carrots and garlic. Pour broth over carrots in cooker. Top with meat.

3. Cover and cook on low-heat setting for 7 to 8 hours or on high-heat setting for 3½ to 4 hours. If no heat setting is available, cook for 5 to 5½ hours.

4. If using low-heat setting, turn to high-heat setting (if no heat setting is available, continue cooking). Add cabbage. Cover and cook for 30 minutes more. Using a slotted spoon, transfer meat and vegetables to a serving platter.
MAKES 2 SERVINGS

Pot Roast with Chipotle-Fruit Sauce

PREP: 25 minutes
SLOW COOK: 10 hours (low) or 5 hours (high)

NUTRITION FACTS PER SERVING

Calories 288
Fat 7 g
Cholesterol 111 mg
Sodium 140 mg
Carbohydrates 18 g
Fiber 1 g
Protein 38 g

1   3-pound boneless beef chuck pot roast
2   teaspoons garlic-pepper seasoning
1   7-ounce package mixed dried fruit
½   cup water
1   tablespoon finely chopped canned chipotle peppers in adobo sauce (see tip, page 57)
1   tablespoon cold water
2   teaspoons cornstarch
    Hot cooked couscous (optional)

1. Trim fat from roast. If necessary, cut roast to fit in a 3½- or 4-quart slow cooker. Sprinkle both sides of roast with garlic-pepper seasoning. Place roast in the cooker. Add fruit, the ½ cup water, and the chipotle peppers.

2. Cover and cook on low-heat setting for 10 to 11 hours or on high-heat setting for 5 to 5½ hours.

3. Transfer roast and fruit to a serving platter; cover to keep warm. Transfer cooking liquid to a bowl or measuring cup; skim off fat. For sauce, in a medium saucepan combine the 1 tablespoon cold water and the cornstarch; add cooking liquid. Cook and stir over medium heat until thickened and bubbly; cook and stir for 2 minutes more. To serve, spoon sauce over meat and fruit. If desired, serve over hot cooked couscous. **MAKES 8 SERVINGS**

Braised Beef and Root Vegetables with Butternut Squash Polenta

PREP: 30 minutes   BAKE: 2 hours
COOK: 25 minutes   OVEN: 325°F

NUTRITION FACTS PER SERVING

Calories 379   *Fat* 11 g   *Cholesterol* 100 mg   *Sodium* 430 mg   *Carbohydrates* 31 g   *Fiber* 4 g   *Protein* 36 g

2   pounds boneless beef chuck shoulder pot roast
4   teaspoons olive oil
2   stalks celery, cut into 2-inch pieces
2   medium carrots, cut into 2-inch pieces
2   medium parsnips (about 12 ounces), peeled and cut into 2-inch pieces
½   cup coarsely chopped onion (1 medium)
½   of a medium turnip, peeled and cut into 2-inch pieces (about 4 ounces)
½   of a small rutabaga, peeled and cut into 2-inch pieces (about 4 ounces)
½   cup dry red wine or reduced-sodium beef broth
2   teaspoons snipped fresh rosemary
1½ cups water
1   cup lower-sodium beef broth
2   teaspoons Kitchen Bouquet
⅓   cup fat-free milk
¼   cup water
1   cup cold water
¾   cup yellow cornmeal
½   of a 10-ounce package frozen butternut squash (⅔ cup), thawed
½   teaspoon salt
¼   teaspoon ground black pepper
¼   cup cold water
1½ tablespoons all-purpose flour
   Fresh parsley leaves

1. Preheat oven to 325°F. Trim fat from beef. Cut meat into 1½-inch pieces. In a 4-quart ovenproof Dutch oven heat 2 teaspoons of the oil over medium heat. Cook meat, half at a time, until browned, stirring frequently. Remove meat from Dutch oven.

2. In the same Dutch oven cook celery, carrots, parsnips, onion, turnip, and rutabaga in the remaining oil for 5 to 7 minutes, until vegetables start to brown. Remove from heat. Stir in wine and rosemary. Add the 1½ cups water, broth, and Kitchen Bouquet; cook and stir over medium heat until boiling, stirring to scrape up any browned bits from bottom of Dutch oven.

3. Bake, covered, about 2 hours or until meat is tender.

4. Meanwhile, for polenta, in a medium saucepan combine milk and ¼ cup water; bring to boiling. In a medium bowl stir together the 1 cup cold water and cornmeal. Slowly add the cornmeal mixture to the boiling milk mixture. Reduce heat to medium low. Stir in squash, salt, and pepper. Cook for 25 to 30 minutes or until polenta is thick and tender, stirring frequently and adjusting heat as needed to maintain a slow boil.

5. Stir together ¼ cup cold water and flour. Add to meat mixture. Cook and stir over medium heat until thickened and bubbly; cook and stir for 1 minute more.

6. Spoon polenta into shallow serving bowls. Top with braised meat and vegetables. Sprinkle with parsley leaves. **MAKES 6 SERVINGS**

Asian Beef Cabbage Wraps

PREP: 20 minutes
SLOW COOK: 8 hours (low) or 4 hours (high) + 15 minutes (high)

NUTRITION FACTS PER CABBAGE WRAP OR 2 LETTUCE WRAPS

Calories 214
Fat 12 g
Cholesterol 65 mg
Sodium 413 mg
Carbohydrates 6 g
Fiber 2 g
Protein 20 g

1   2¾- to 3-pound boneless beef chuck pot roast
1½ cups chopped, peeled jicama or chopped celery
½   cup chopped green onions (4)
¼   cup rice vinegar
¼   cup reduced-sodium soy sauce
2   tablespoons hoisin sauce
1   tablespoon grated fresh ginger
½   teaspoon salt
½   teaspoon chile oil
¼   teaspoon ground black pepper
2   tablespoons cornstarch
2   tablespoons cold water
12   savoy cabbage leaves or 24 butterhead (Boston or Bibb) lettuce leaves
¼   cup coarsely chopped cashews (optional)
     Jicama strips (optional)
     Slivered green onions (optional)
     Crushed red pepper

1. Trim fat from meat. If necessary, cut meat to fit into a 3½- or 4-quart slow cooker. Place meat in the cooker. In a medium bowl combine jicama, green onions, vinegar, soy sauce, hoisin sauce, ginger, salt, chile oil, and black pepper. Pour over meat.

2. Cover and cook on low-heat setting for 8 to 10 hours or on high-heat setting for 4 to 5 hours.

3. If using low-heat setting, turn cooker to high-heat setting. In a small bowl combine cornstarch and the cold water; stir into liquid and meat mixture in cooker. Cover and cook about 15 minutes more or until thickened.

4. Remove meat from cooker, reserving cooking juices. Using two forks, pull meat apart into shreds.

5. Spoon shredded meat onto cabbage or lettuce leaves. If desired, top with cashews, jicama strips, and/or slivered green onions. Sprinkle with crushed red pepper. Fold cabbage or lettuce leaves around filling; roll and secure with cocktail picks. Serve wraps with reserved cooking juices for dipping. **MAKES 12 SERVINGS**

Meat Loaf with Sour Cream- Mushroom Sauce

PREP: 35 minutes
BAKE: 1 hour
STAND: 10 minutes
OVEN: 350°F

NUTRITION FACTS PER SERVING

Calories 214
Fat 10 g
Cholesterol 65 mg
Sodium 534 mg
Carbohydrates 10 g
Fiber 1 g
Protein 21 g

⅓ cup fat-free milk
2 egg whites
1 cup soft whole grain bread crumbs (1⅓ slices)
¼ cup chopped green onions (2)
2 teaspoons dried Italian seasoning, crushed
¼ teaspoon salt
⅛ teaspoon ground black pepper
1 pound 95% lean ground beef
   Nonstick cooking spray
1 tablespoon butter
1½ cups sliced fresh mushrooms
1 clove garlic, minced
¼ cup thinly sliced green onions (2)
1 8-ounce carton light sour cream
2 tablespoons all-purpose flour
¾ cup cold water
2 teaspoons instant beef bouillon granules
   Sliced green onions (optional)
   Ground black pepper (optional)

1. Preheat oven to 350°F. Line a 2-quart rectangular baking dish with foil; set aside.

2. In a large bowl combine milk and egg whites; beat with a fork until well mixed. Stir in bread crumbs, ¼ cup chopped green onions, the Italian seasoning, salt, and the ⅛ teaspoon pepper. Add ground beef; mix well. Shape beef mixture into a 7×4-inch rectangle in the prepared baking dish.

3. Bake about 1 hour or until internal temperature reaches 160°F.* Spoon off fat. Let meat loaf stand for 10 minutes. Using two spatulas, carefully transfer meat loaf to serving platter, draining off as much fat as possible.

4. Meanwhile, for sour cream sauce, coat a medium skillet with cooking spray. Add butter; melt over medium heat. Add mushrooms and garlic; cook about 4 minutes or until mushrooms are nearly tender. Stir in ¼ cup sliced green onions; cook for 1 minute more. In a small bowl stir together sour cream and flour. Stir the cold water and bouillon granules into the mushroom mixture. Stir sour cream mixture into mushroom mixture in skillet. Cook and stir until thickened and bubbly. Cook and stir for 1 minute more. Add additional water if needed to thin to desired consistency. Serve sauce over meat loaf. If desired, sprinkle with additional sliced green onions and pepper. **MAKES 6 SERVINGS**

*Tip: The internal color of meat loaf is not a reliable doneness indicator. A beef loaf cooked to 160°F is safe, regardless of color. To measure doneness, insert an instant-read thermometer into the center of the loaf.

Zesty Meat Sauce with Spaghetti Squash

PREP: 50 minutes   BAKE: 45 minutes
OVEN: 350°F

NUTRITION FACTS PER SERVING

Calories 181   *Fat* 4 g   *Cholesterol* 37 mg   *Sodium* 236 mg   *Carbohydrates* 21 g   *Fiber* 6 g   *Protein* 16 g

1   medium spaghetti squash (about 2½ pounds)
1   medium red or green sweet pepper,* stemmed, seeded, and cut into thin strips
4   ounces fresh mushrooms, quartered
1   small onion, cut into thin wedges
    Nonstick cooking spray
12 ounces 95% lean ground beef
½   cup chopped onion (1 medium)
½   cup chopped carrot (1 medium)
½   cup chopped celery (1 stalk)
2   cloves garlic, minced
2   8-ounce cans no-salt-added tomato sauce
1   cup salsa**
1   cup water
1   tablespoon dried Italian seasoning, crushed
¼   teaspoon ground black pepper
⅛   to ¼ teaspoon crushed red pepper
¼   cup finely shredded Parmesan cheese

1. Preheat oven to 350°F. Line a 15×10×1-inch baking pan with foil. Halve squash lengthwise. Remove seeds. Place squash, cut sides down, in prepared baking pan. Using a fork, prick the skin all over. Arrange sweet pepper, mushrooms, and onion wedges around squash. Coat vegetables with cooking spray. Bake for 45 to 55 minutes or until squash is tender.

2. Meanwhile, for meat sauce, in a large skillet combine ground beef, chopped onion, carrot, celery, and garlic. Cook until meat is browned and vegetables are tender, using a wooden spoon to break up meat as it cooks. Drain well.

3. Stir tomato sauce, salsa, the water, Italian seasoning, black pepper, and crushed red pepper into meat sauce in skillet. Bring to boiling; reduce heat. Simmer, uncovered, for 10 to 15 minutes or until desired consistency, stirring occasionally.

4. Using a fork, remove squash pulp from shells. In a large bowl toss 4 cups*** of the squash with the roasted sweet pepper strips, mushrooms, and onion wedges.

5. Serve meat sauce over squash-vegetable mixture. Sprinkle with cheese. **MAKES 6 SERVINGS**

*Tip: For added color, use half of a red sweet pepper and half of a green sweet pepper.

**Tip: Read nutritional facts on salsa labels to choose the salsa lowest in sodium. Newman's Own Mild Salsa is a good choice for low sodium.

***Tip: Refrigerate any leftover squash in a covered container for up to 3 days. Serve with pesto or pasta sauce as a side dish.

Glazed Teriyaki Pork Chops with Potatoes

PREP: 20 minutes
BROIL: 6 minutes

NUTRITION FACTS
PER SERVING

Calories 394
Fat 15 g
Cholesterol 86 mg
Sodium 626 mg
Carbohydrates 23 g
Fiber 2 g
Protein 38 g

4   boneless pork loin chops, cut
    ¾ inch thick
¼   cup bottled teriyaki glaze
12 ounces tiny new potatoes,
    quartered
1   tablespoon olive oil
1   tablespoon toasted sesame oil
¼   teaspoon salt
⅛   teaspoon ground black pepper
1   cup fresh pea pods, halved
    lengthwise
    Bottled teriyaki glaze
    (optional)

1. Preheat broiler. Brush both sides of chops with the ¼ cup teriyaki glaze. Arrange chops on half of the unheated rack of a broiler pan; set aside.

2. Place potatoes in a large bowl. Drizzle potatoes with olive oil, and sesame oil; sprinkle with salt and pepper; toss to coat. Arrange potatoes in a single layer on the rack next to chops.

3. Broil 3 to 4 inches from heat for 6 to 8 minutes or until chops are done (145°F) and potatoes are tender, turning the pork and potatoes once halfway through broiling.

4. Place pea pods in a large bowl. Add potatoes; toss to combine. Serve pork with potatoes and pea pods. Pass additional teriyaki glaze. **MAKES 4 SERVINGS**

Grilled Pork and Pineapple

START TO FINISH: 20 minutes

4 boneless pork top loin chops, cut ¾ inch thick (about 1¼ pounds total)
¼ teaspoon salt
¼ teaspoon ground black pepper
1 purchased peeled and cored fresh pineapple
3 tablespoons orange marmalade
½ cup plain yogurt
¼ cup coarsely chopped roasted, lightly salted cashews
Fresh thyme sprigs (optional)

1. Trim fat from pork chops. Sprinkle both sides of chops with the salt and pepper. Cut pineapple crosswise into ½-inch slices; set aside.

2. For a charcoal or gas grill, place chops on the grill rack directly over medium heat. Grill, uncovered, for 3 minutes. Turn; add pineapple to grill. Brush chops and pineapple with 1 tablespoon marmalade. Grill for 3 to 5 minutes more or until chops are done (145°F) and pineapple has light grill marks, turning pineapple once and brushing with any remaining marmalade. Let chops rest for 3 minutes.

3. Arrange pineapple and chops on serving plates. Combine yogurt and 2 tablespoons of the marmalade. Spoon yogurt mixture over chops and pineapple; sprinkle with cashews. If desired, garnish with fresh thyme. **MAKES 4 SERVINGS**

Grilled Pork Chops with Chile Rub and Chutney

START TO FINISH: 30 minutes

NUTRITION FACTS PER SERVING

Calories 289   *Fat* 14 g   *Cholesterol* 78 mg   *Sodium* 207 mg   *Carbohydrates* 16 g   *Fiber* 3 g   *Protein* 25 g

1   tablespoon olive oil
1   medium sweet onion, such as Vidalia or Walla Walla, thinly sliced
½   teaspoon cumin seeds
¼   teaspoon sea salt
4   pork loin chops,* cut ¾ inch thick (about 2 pounds total)
1   large chipotle pepper in adobo sauce, finely chopped**
2   oranges, peeled, seeded, and sectioned
¼   cup orange juice

1. In a large skillet heat oil over medium heat. Add onion, cumin seeds, and sea salt; cook for 12 to 15 minutes or until onion is tender and golden brown, stirring occasionally.

2. Meanwhile, trim fat from pork chops. Rub chopped chipotle pepper onto chops.**

3. For a charcoal or gas grill, grill chops on the rack of a covered grill directly over medium heat for 6 to 8 minutes or until done (145°F), turning once halfway through grilling.

4. Add orange sections and orange juice to onion mixture. Bring to boiling; reduce heat. Simmer, uncovered, for 5 minutes, stirring occasionally. Serve over grilled pork chops. **MAKES 4 SERVINGS**

*Tip: If using pork chops that have not been injected with a sodium solution, sprinkle chops with ¼ teaspoon sea salt before grilling.

**Tip: Because chile peppers contain volatile oils that can burn your skin and eyes, avoid direct contact with them as much as possible. When working with chile peppers, wear plastic or rubber gloves. If your bare hands do touch the chile peppers, wash your hands and fingernails well with soap and water.

Apricot Pork with Garlic Green Beans

START TO FINISH: 20 minutes

NUTRITION FACTS
PER SERVING

Calories 295
Fat 14 g
Cholesterol 57 mg
Sodium 207 mg
Carbohydrates 20 g
Fiber 4 g
Protein 22 g

4   pork rib chops, cut ½ inch thick
    Salt
    Ground black pepper
1   tablespoon olive oil
4   apricots, pitted and cut into wedges
2   tablespoons honey
3   cloves garlic, sliced
1   pound green beans, trimmed if desired

1. Trim fat from chops. Lightly sprinkle chops with salt and pepper. In an extra-large nonstick skillet heat the oil over medium-high heat; reduce heat to medium. Cook chops in hot oil for 3 minutes, turning once. Add apricots, honey, and garlic to skillet. Cover and cook for 3 to 5 minutes or until apricots are tender and pork is done (145°F).

2. Meanwhile, in a 2-quart microwave-safe bowl combine beans and the ¼ cup water. Cover with vented plastic wrap. Microwave on 100 percent power (high) for 6 minutes, stirring once; drain.

3. Serve pork and apricots with green beans. Spoon cooking juices from skillet over all.
MAKES 4 SERVINGS

Pork Tenderloin with Cucumber-Mango Salad

PREP: 5 minutes
ROAST: 20 minutes
STAND: 5 minutes
OVEN: 425°F

NUTRITION FACTS PER SERVING

Calories 258
Fat 3 g
Cholesterol 110 mg
Sodium 370 mg
Carbohydrates 19 g
Fiber 2 g
Protein 37 g

2   tablespoons packed brown sugar
2   teaspoons five-spice powder
½   teaspoon salt
1½ pounds pork tenderloin
4   green onions
1   mango, peeled, seeded, and chopped
1   small English cucumber, sliced and/or chopped
1   jalapeño pepper, seeded and sliced (see tip, page 114) (optional)

1. Preheat oven to 425°F. In a small bowl combine brown sugar, five-spice powder, and salt. Set aside 1 teaspoon brown sugar mixture to use in salad. Rub the remaining brown sugar mixture onto pork tenderloin. Place tenderloin in a foil-lined baking pan.

2. Roast, uncovered, about 20 minutes or until a meat thermometer registers 140°F. Cover with foil and let stand for 5 minutes (meat temperature will rise to 145°F).

3. Meanwhile, for cucumber-mango salad, slice the green portion of green onions into thin strips; chop the white portion. In a medium bowl combine green onions, mango, cucumber, jalapeño pepper (if desired), and the reserved brown sugar mixture.

4. Slice pork and serve with cucumber-mango salad.
MAKES 4 SERVINGS

Cocoa Roasted Pork with Wilted Kale

PREP: 25 minutes   ROAST: 20 minutes
STAND: 3 minutes   OVEN: 425°F

NUTRITION FACTS PER SERVING

Calories 286   *Fat* 7 g   *Cholesterol* 1 mg   *Sodium* 429 mg   *Carbohydrates* 29 g   *Fiber* 6 g   *Protein* 30 g

1   cup water
1   tablespoon packed brown sugar
1   teaspoon instant espresso coffee powder
1   teaspoon unsweetened cocoa powder
½   teaspoon salt
½   teaspoon ground ancho chile pepper
1   1-pound pork tenderloin, trimmed of fat
1   medium red sweet pepper, cut into thin bite-size strips
1   large onion, thinly sliced
1   tablespoon olive oil
12   cups coarsely chopped, trimmed kale

1. Preheat oven to 425°F. Place a rack in a shallow roasting pan. Pour the water into the pan; set aside. For rub, in a small bowl combine brown sugar, coffee powder, cocoa powder, ¼ teaspoon of the salt, and the ancho chile pepper. Sprinkle rub evenly over pork; rub in with your fingers. Place pork on the rack in the prepared pan.

2. Roast for 20 to 30 minutes or until an instant-read thermometer inserted in center of pork registers 145°F. Cover pork with foil. Let stand for 3 minutes before slicing.

3. Meanwhile, in a Dutch oven cook sweet pepper and onion in hot oil over medium heat about 5 minutes or until crisp-tender, stirring occasionally. Add kale; sprinkle with the remaining ¼ teaspoon salt. Cook for 3 to 5 minutes or until kale is tender, tossing with tongs for kale to cook evenly. Thinly slice pork. Serve with wilted kale. **MAKES 4 SERVINGS**

Thai Pork and Vegetable Curry

START TO FINISH: 30 minutes

NUTRITION FACTS
PER SERVING

Calories 481
Fat 16 g
Cholesterol 55 mg
Sodium 464 mg
Carbohydrates 62 g
Fiber 4 g
Protein 23 g

1⅓ cups uncooked jasmine rice
    (about 9 ounces)
12 ounces pork tenderloin or lean
    boneless pork
    Salt
    Ground black pepper
2   tablespoons canola oil
8   ounces fresh green beans*
    (2 cups)
1   medium red sweet pepper, cut
    into thin bite-size strips
2   green onions, bias-sliced into
    ¼-inch pieces
1   14-ounce can unsweetened
    light coconut milk
4   teaspoons bottled curry paste
1   teaspoon sugar
⅛   teaspoon crushed red pepper
1   lime, cut into wedges

1. Cook rice according to package directions. Keep warm.

2. Meanwhile, thinly slice pork into bite-size pieces. Sprinkle with salt and pepper. In a large nonstick skillet heat 1 tablespoon of the oil over medium-high heat. Add pork; cook and stir about 4 minutes or until no pink remains. Remove pork from skillet.

3. Add the remaining 1 tablespoon oil to skillet. Add green beans; cook and stir for 3 minutes. Add sweet pepper and green onions; cook and stir about 2 minutes more or until vegetables are crisp-tender. Remove from skillet.

Add coconut milk, curry paste, sugar, and crushed red pepper to skillet. Bring to boiling; reduce heat. Simmer, uncovered, about 2 minutes or until curry mixture is slightly thickened. Stir in pork and vegetables; heat through. Serve with hot cooked rice and lime wedges.
MAKES 4 SERVINGS

*Tip: A 9-ounce package of frozen green beans, thawed, may be substituted for the fresh beans. Add them to the skillet along with the sweet pepper and onions; cook as directed.

Garlic Pork and Sweet Potato Hash

START TO FINISH: 30 minutes

NUTRITION FACTS PER SERVING

Calories 451
Fat 16 g
Cholesterol 107 mg
Sodium 449 mg
Carbohydrates 39 g
Fiber 4 g
Protein 37 g

4   cups chopped sweet potatoes (3 small)
1½ pounds pork tenderloin, cut into 1-inch slices
2   tablespoons reduced-sodium soy sauce
    Ground black pepper
3   tablespoons canola oil
8   cloves garlic, peeled and thinly sliced
¼   cup sliced green onions (2)
2   tablespoons honey
2   tablespoons water

1. Place sweet potatoes in a microwave-safe bowl; cover with vented plastic wrap. Microwave on 100 percent power (high) for 8 minutes, stirring once. Carefully remove plastic wrap; set aside.

2. Meanwhile, to butterfly pork slices, cut three-quarters through each; open and flatten slightly. Brush with 1 tablespoon of the soy sauce; lightly sprinkle with black pepper.

3. In an extra-large skillet heat oil over medium-high heat. Add garlic; cook just until it begins to turn golden.* Remove garlic and set aside. Add pork to the skillet. Cook for 4 to 6 minutes or until done (145°F), turning once halfway through cooking. Transfer pork to a platter; cover to keep meat warm.

4. For hash, add partially cooked sweet potatoes to the skillet. Cook until potatoes begin to crisp, stirring occasionally. Add green onions; cook for 1 minute. Spoon hash onto plates; top with pork and garlic.

5. For sauce, in the hot skillet whisk together honey, water, and the remaining 1 tablespoon soy sauce; cook just until bubbly. Drizzle sauce over pork. **MAKES 4 SERVINGS**

*****Tip:** Cook the garlic just until golden, not brown. Burned garlic has a bitter taste.

Zucchini-Wrapped Pork

PREP: 12 minutes
ROAST: 18 minutes
OVEN: 450°F

NUTRITION FACTS PER SERVING

Calories 203   *Fat* 11 g   *Cholesterol* 62 mg   *Sodium* 382 mg   *Carbohydrates* 4 g   *Fiber* 1 g   *Protein* 21 g

1   small zucchini
1   12-ounce pork tenderloin
    Olive oil
    Salt
    Ground black pepper
⅓   cup purchased basil pesto
    Small fresh basil leaves
    Watercress or arugula
    (optional)

1. Preheat oven to 450°F. Line a 15×10×1-inch baking pan with foil; set aside. With a sharp knife or vegetable peeler, cut zucchini lengthwise into thin slices (you'll need 8 slices). Cut pork tenderloin crosswise into 4 equal portions. Press meat with the palm of your hand to flatten slightly.

2. Wrap each tenderloin portion with two zucchini slices (reserve remaining zucchini for another use). Place in prepared pan. Lightly brush with oil; sprinkle with salt and pepper.

3. Roast, uncovered, for 18 to 20 minutes or until an instant-read meat thermometer inserted in center of meat registers 145°F. Spoon some of the pesto over meat and sprinkle with basil leaves. Serve with the remaining pesto and, if desired, watercress.
MAKES 4 SERVINGS

Pork-Wasabi Tacos

PREP: 15 minutes
GRILL: 10 minutes

NUTRITION FACTS
PER TACO

Calories 447
Fat 13 g
Cholesterol 89 mg
Sodium 470 mg
Carbohydrates 50 g
Fiber 2 g
Protein 31 g

1	1½-pound pork tenderloin, cut into 1-inch pieces
⅓	cup hoisin sauce
6	flatbreads or flour tortillas
1	to 2 teaspoons prepared wasabi paste
2	tablespoons water
2	tablespoons canola oil
½	teaspoon white wine vinegar
½	teaspoon sugar
¼	of a head napa cabbage, shredded
2	carrots, shredded
½	English cucumber, thinly sliced

1. Thread pork on skewers.* Brush with hoisin sauce. For a charcoal or gas grill, grill pork on the rack of a covered grill directly over medium heat for 10 to 12 minutes or until done (145°F), turning once halfway through grilling. Add flatbreads the last 1 minute of grilling time, turning once to heat through.

2. Meanwhile, for wasabi oil, in a small bowl whisk together wasabi paste, water, oil, vinegar, and sugar.

3. Serve pork, shredded cabbage, carrots, and cucumber slices on flatbreads. Drizzle with wasabi oil. Serve immediately. **MAKES 6 TACOS**

*Tip: If using wooden skewers, soak in enough water to cover for at least 1 hour before using.

Asian Pork and Noodle Skillet

START TO FINISH: 20 minutes

NUTRITION FACTS PER SERVING

Calories 312
Fat 15 g
Cholesterol 54 mg
Sodium 646 mg
Carbohydrates 21 g
Fiber 2 g
Protein 23 g

2   tablespoons canola oil
12   ounces boneless pork, trimmed of fat and cut into bite-size strips
1½ cups water
1   3-ounce package oriental- or pork-flavor ramen noodles, broken
2   cups fresh snow pea pods
2   orange, red, and/or yellow sweet peppers, cut into bite-size strips
2   tablespoons hoisin sauce
     Ground black pepper

1. In a large skillet heat oil over medium-high heat. Add pork; cook and stir about 2 minutes or until lightly browned.

2. Add the water to skillet; bring to boiling. Add noodles and seasoning packet, snow peas, sweet peppers, and hoisin sauce. Return to boiling; reduce heat. Simmer, covered, for 5 minutes. Season with black pepper. **MAKES 4 SERVINGS**

Fennel and Pork Sausage with Grape Relish

PREP: 15 minutes
GRILL: 14 minutes

NUTRITION FACTS PER SERVING

Calories 284   *Fat* 14 g   *Cholesterol* 106 mg   *Sodium* 409 mg   *Carbohydrates* 23 g   *Fiber* 7 g   *Protein* 18 g

1   egg, lightly beaten
1   tablespoon bourbon (optional)
½   cup quick-cooking rolled oats
1   tablespoon fennel seeds, crushed
1   teaspoon finely shredded lemon peel
1   teaspoon paprika
½   teaspoon salt
½   teaspoon ground black pepper
1   clove garlic, minced
1   pound lean ground pork
1½ cups red seedless grapes, halved
1   cup coarsely chopped fennel (1 medium bulb)
1   tablespoon butter
2   tablespoons balsamic vinegar
4   slices bread, toasted (optional)
¼   cup snipped fresh parsley

1. In a large bowl combine the egg and, if desired, bourbon. Stir in rolled oats, fennel seeds, lemon peel, paprika, salt, pepper, and garlic. Add ground pork; mix well. Shape the pork mixture into four ¾-inch-thick patties. Set aside.

2. Fold a 36×18-inch piece of heavy foil in half to make a double thickness of foil that measures 18 inches square. Place the grapes, fennel, butter, and vinegar in the center of the foil. Sprinkle with additional salt and pepper. Bring up two opposite edges of foil and seal with a double fold. Fold remaining edges to completely enclose grape relish, leaving space for steam to build.

3. For a charcoal or gas grill, place pork patties and foil packet on grill rack over medium heat. Grill, covered, for 14 to 16 minutes or until no pink remains in the patties (160°F),* turning once.

4. If desired, serve pork patties on bread. Carefully open packet and spoon grape relish over the grilled patties. Sprinkle with the fresh parsley. MAKES 4 SERVINGS

*Tip: The internal color of a burger is not a reliable doneness indicator. A beef or pork patty cooked to 160°F is safe, regardless of color. To test for doneness, insert an instant-read thermometer through the side of the burger to a depth of 2 to 3 inches.

Tomato-Topped Lamb Chops and Rice

START TO FINISH: 20 minutes

NUTRITION FACTS PER SERVING

Calories 273
Fat 7 g
Cholesterol 70 mg
Sodium 153 mg
Carbohydrates 26 g
Fiber 3 g
Protein 25 g

8   lamb loin chops, cut 1 inch thick
    Salt
    Ground black pepper
1   8.8-ounce pouch cooked long grain rice
4   roma tomatoes, cut up
4   green onions, cut into 1-inch pieces
1   tablespoon snipped fresh oregano
1   tablespoon balsamic vinegar

1. Trim fat from chops. Sprinkle chops with salt and pepper. For a charcoal or gas grill, grill chops on the rack of a covered grill directly over medium heat for 12 to 14 minutes for medium rare (145°F) or 15 to 17 minutes for medium (160°F), turning once halfway through grilling time.

2. Meanwhile, heat rice in a microwave oven according to package directions. In a food processor combine tomatoes, green onions, and oregano. Cover and process with on/off pulses to coarsely chop. Transfer to a small bowl; stir in balsamic vinegar. Season with additional salt and pepper.

3. Divide rice among four dinner plates; top with chops. Serve with tomato mixture. **MAKES 4 SERVINGS**

CHAPTER 6

Poultry

Lickety-Split Lemon Chicken

START TO FINISH: 30 minutes

NUTRITION FACTS
PER SERVING

Calories 361
Fat 10 g
Cholesterol 66 mg
Sodium 643 mg
Carbohydrates 41 g
Fiber 2 g
Protein 25 g

2   tablespoons butter
12   ounces chicken breast
     tenderloins
1   8-ounce package sliced fresh
     mushrooms
1   medium red sweet pepper, cut
     into bite-size pieces
2   tablespoons all-purpose flour
1   14.5-ounce can chicken broth
1   teaspoon finely shredded
     lemon peel
2   tablespoons lemon juice
1   teaspoon dried thyme,
     crushed
     Salt
     Ground black pepper
1   8.8-ounce package cooked
     long grain white rice
     Lemon wedges (optional)

1. In an extra-large skillet melt butter over medium heat. Add chicken; cook for 6 to 8 minutes or until no longer pink (170°F), adding mushrooms and sweet pepper for the last 5 minutes of cooking time. Stir in flour. Cook and stir for 1 minute more. Add broth, lemon peel, lemon juice, and thyme. Cook and stir until thickened and bubbly. Cook and stir for 2 minutes more. Season with salt and black pepper.

2. Meanwhile, prepare rice according to package directions. Serve lemon chicken over rice. If desired, serve with lemon wedges.
MAKES 4 SERVINGS

Arroz con Pollo

START TO FINISH: 25 minutes

NUTRITION FACTS PER SERVING

Calories 399
Fat 14 g
Cholesterol 102 mg
Sodium 939 mg
Carbohydrates 29 g
Fiber 4 g
Protein 37 g

1   purchased roasted chicken
1   14.5-ounce can diced
    tomatoes, undrained
1   4-ounce can diced green
    chiles, undrained
1   cup frozen peas
⅓   cup pitted green olives, sliced
1   8.8-ounce pouch cooked
    Spanish-style rice
⅓   cup shredded Monterey Jack
    cheese

1. Remove chicken meat from bones, discarding skin and bones. Tear chicken into large pieces. Measure 3 cups of the chicken; save remaining chicken for another use.

2. In a large skillet combine tomatoes, green chiles, peas, and olives. Bring to boiling. Stir in rice and the 3 cups chicken; heat through. Top each serving with cheese. **MAKES 4 SERVINGS**

Chicken Curry Skillet with Rice Noodles

START TO FINISH: 30 minutes

NUTRITION FACTS PER SERVING

Calories 386   *Fat* 10 g   *Cholesterol* 66 mg   *Sodium* 529 mg   *Carbohydrates* 42 g   *Fiber* 2 g   *Protein* 28 g

8   ounces wide rice noodles, broken
2   tablespoons canola oil
1½ pounds skinless, boneless chicken breast, cut into 1-inch pieces
1   16-ounce package frozen stir-fry vegetables, thawed
1   14-ounce can unsweetened light coconut milk
½   cup water
1   tablespoon sugar
1   tablespoon fish sauce
½   to 1 teaspoon red curry paste
¼   teaspoon salt
¼   teaspoon ground black pepper
¼   cup snipped fresh basil

1. Soak rice noodles according to package directions; drain.

2. Meanwhile, in an extra-large skillet heat oil over medium-high heat. Add chicken; cook and stir for 8 to 10 minutes or until chicken is no longer pink, adding stir-fry vegetables for the last 4 minutes of cooking. Remove chicken mixture from skillet.

3. In the same skillet combine coconut milk, the water, sugar, fish sauce, curry paste, salt, and pepper. Bring to boiling. Stir in rice noodles and chicken mixture. Return to boiling; reduce heat. Simmer, uncovered, about 2 minutes or until noodles are tender but still firm and sauce is thickened. Sprinkle with basil. **MAKES 6 SERVINGS**

Tex-Mex Chicken 'n' Rice Casserole

PREP: 20 minutes
CHILL: 2 hours
BAKE: 30 minutes
STAND: 5 minutes
OVEN: 425°F

NUTRITION FACTS PER SERVING

Calories 323
Fat 14 g
Cholesterol 53 mg
Sodium 971 mg
Carbohydrates 30 g
Fiber 2 g
Protein 21 g

1   tablespoon olive oil
½   cup chopped onion
    (1 medium)
1   6.9-ounce package chicken-
    flavor rice and vermicelli mix
2   cups water
1   14.5-ounce can chicken broth
2   cups chopped cooked chicken
    (10 ounces)
1   cup chopped, seeded
    tomatoes (2 medium)
3   tablespoons canned diced
    green chiles, drained
1½ teaspoons chili powder
1   teaspoon dried basil, crushed
⅛   teaspoon ground cumin
⅛   teaspoon ground black pepper
½   cup shredded cheddar cheese
    (2 ounces)

1. In a medium saucepan heat oil over medium heat. Add onion; cook until tender, stirring occasionally. Stir in rice and vermicelli mix (including contents of the seasoning packet). Cook and stir for 2 minutes. Stir in the water and broth. Bring to boiling; reduce heat. Simmer, covered, for 20 minutes (liquid will not be fully absorbed).

2. Transfer rice mixture to a large bowl. Stir in chicken, tomatoes, chiles, chili powder, basil, cumin, and pepper. Transfer to an ungreased 2-quart casserole. Cover with foil and chill for 2 to 24 hours.

3. Preheat oven to 425°F. Bake, covered, for 30 to 35 minutes or until heated through. Sprinkle with cheese. Let stand for 5 minutes before serving. **MAKES 6 SERVINGS**

Thai Green Chicken Curry

START TO FINISH: 30 minutes

NUTRITION FACTS PER SERVING

Calories 344
Fat 13 g
Cholesterol 81 mg
Sodium 445 mg
Carbohydrates 37 g
Fiber 4 g
Protein 21 g

12   ounces skinless, boneless chicken thighs
1   cup canned unsweetened light coconut milk
¼   cup reduced-sodium chicken broth
2   to 3 tablespoons green curry paste
2   teaspoons cornstarch
2   teaspoons finely chopped fresh lemongrass or 1 teaspoon finely shredded lemon peel
     Nonstick cooking spray
1   medium green sweet pepper, seeded and cut into thin bite-size strips (1 cup)
1   medium onion, halved and thinly sliced
¾   cup packaged shredded fresh carrots
3   cloves garlic, minced
2   teaspoons canola oil
2   cups hot cooked brown basmati rice or regular brown rice
¼   cup flaked coconut, toasted*
     Fresh cilantro sprigs

1. Trim fat from chicken. Cut chicken into thin bite-size strips; set aside. For sauce, in a medium bowl whisk together coconut milk, broth, curry paste, cornstarch, and lemon peel (if using); set aside.

2. Coat a wok or large nonstick skillet with cooking spray; heat wok over medium-high heat. Add sweet pepper and onion; cook and stir for 3 minutes. Add carrots, garlic, and lemongrass (if using); cook and stir about 2 minutes or until vegetables are crisp-tender. Remove vegetables from wok.

3. Add oil to wok; add chicken. Cook and stir over medium-high heat for 3 to 5 minutes or until chicken is no longer pink. Push chicken from center of wok.

4. Stir sauce; pour into center of wok. Cook and stir until slightly thickened and bubbly. Return vegetables to wok; stir all ingredients together to coat with sauce. Cook and stir about 2 minutes or until heated through.

5. Serve chicken curry over rice. Sprinkle with coconut and cilantro.
MAKES 4 SERVINGS

*Tip: To toast coconut, spread it in a shallow baking pan. Bake in 350°F oven about 5 minutes or until golden, shaking pan once or twice. Watch carefully to prevent coconut from burning.

Grilled Chicken and Peaches with Green Beans and Orzo

START TO FINISH: 30 minutes

NUTRITION FACTS PER SERVING

Calories 526   *Fat* 17 g   *Cholesterol* 93 mg   *Sodium* 604 mg   *Carbohydrates* 55 g   *Fiber* 5 g   *Protein* 38 g

8   ounces dried orzo (1⅓ cups)
8   ounces green beans, trimmed (about 2½ cups)
1   pound chicken breast tenderloins
2   medium peaches, cut into wedges
2   tablespoons olive oil
¼   teaspoon salt
¼   teaspoon ground black pepper
2   to 4 ounces herb-flavor feta cheese (garlic and herb or peppercorn), crumbled
     Fresh thyme (optional)

1. In a large saucepan or Dutch oven cook orzo according to package directions. Add green beans for the last 5 minutes of cooking time. Drain; do not rinse. Remove green beans; set aside orzo and beans.

2. Meanwhile, lightly brush chicken and peaches with some of the oil; sprinkle with salt and pepper.

3. For a charcoal or gas grill, grill chicken and peaches on the rack of a covered grill directly over medium heat for 4 to 6 minutes or until chicken is no longer pink and peaches are tender.

4. In a large bowl combine orzo, feta cheese, and the remaining olive oil; gently toss to mix. Season with additional salt and pepper.

5. Divide green beans among four serving plates. Top with orzo mixture, chicken, and peaches. If desired, garnish with fresh thyme.
MAKES 4 SERVINGS

Rosemary Chicken with Vegetables

START TO FINISH: 30 minutes

NUTRITION FACTS PER SERVING

Calories 324
Fat 11 g
Cholesterol 93 mg
Sodium 339 mg
Carbohydrates 26 g
Fiber 2 g
Protein 29 g

4	medium skinless, boneless chicken breast halves (1 to 1¼ pounds total)
½	teaspoon lemon-pepper seasoning
2	tablespoons olive oil
4	ounces refrigerated plain or spinach linguine
2	cloves garlic, minced
2	medium zucchini and/or yellow summer squash, cut into ¼-inch slices
½	cup apple juice
2	teaspoons snipped fresh rosemary or ½ teaspoon dried rosemary, crushed
¼	teaspoon salt
2	tablespoons dry white wine or chicken broth
2	teaspoons cornstarch
1	cup halved cherry or grape tomatoes

1. Sprinkle chicken with lemon-pepper seasoning. In a large skillet heat oil over medium high-heat. Add chicken; cook for 8 to 10 minutes or until no longer pink, turning once. Transfer chicken to a platter; cover and keep warm.

2. Meanwhile, cook pasta according to package directions; drain and keep warm.

3. Add garlic to drippings in skillet; cook and stir for 15 seconds. Add zucchini, apple juice, rosemary, and salt. Bring to boiling; reduce heat. Simmer, covered, for 2 minutes.

4. In a small bowl stir together wine and cornstarch; add to skillet. Cook and stir until thickened and bubbly; cook and stir for 2 minutes more. Stir in tomatoes. Serve vegetables and pasta with chicken.
MAKES 4 SERVINGS

Range-Top Chicken, Macaroni, and Cheese

START TO FINISH: 30 minutes

NUTRITION FACTS PER SERVING

Calories 369
Fat 12 g
Cholesterol 85 mg
Sodium 393 mg
Carbohydrates 33 g
Fiber 4 g
Protein 33 g

1½ cups dried multigrain or regular elbow macaroni (6 ounces)
Nonstick cooking spray
12 ounces skinless, boneless chicken breast, cut into 1-inch pieces
¼ cup finely chopped onion
1 6.5-ounce package light semisoft cheese with garlic and herb
1⅔ cups fat-free milk
1 tablespoon all-purpose flour
¾ cup shredded reduced-fat cheddar cheese (3 ounces)
2 cups baby spinach
1 cup cherry tomatoes, quartered

1. In a medium saucepan cook macaroni according to package directions, except do not add salt to the water; drain.

2. Meanwhile, coat a large nonstick skillet with cooking spray; heat skillet over medium-high heat. Add chicken and onion to hot skillet. Cook for 4 to 6 minutes or until chicken is no longer pink and onion is tender, stirring frequently. (If onion browns too quickly, reduce heat to medium.) Remove skillet from heat. Add semisoft cheese; stir until melted.

3. In a medium bowl whisk together milk and flour until smooth. Add all at once to chicken mixture. Cook and stir over medium heat until thickened and bubbly. Reduce heat to low. Add cheddar cheese, stirring until melted. Add cooked macaroni; cook and stir for 1 to 2 minutes or until heated through. Stir in spinach. Top with cherry tomatoes. Serve immediately.

MAKES 5 SERVINGS

Sesame-Ginger Barbecued Chicken

START TO FINISH: **30 minutes**

NUTRITION FACTS PER SERVING

Calories 190   *Fat* 2 g   *Cholesterol* 77 mg   *Sodium* 278 mg   *Carbohydrates* 9 g   *Fiber* 0 g   *Protein* 31 g

⅓   cup plum sauce or sweet-and-sour sauce
¼   cup water
3   tablespoons hoisin sauce
1½ teaspoons sesame seeds, toasted* if desired
1   teaspoon grated fresh ginger or ¼ teaspoon ground ginger
¼   to ½ teaspoon Asian chili sauce (Sriracha sauce) or several dashes bottled hot pepper sauce
1   clove garlic, minced
6   skinless, boneless chicken breast halves or 12 skinless, boneless chicken thighs
    Hot cooked noodles or rice (optional)
    Sesame seeds, toasted* if desired (optional)
    Green onion curls (optional)

1. For sauce, in a small saucepan combine plum sauce, the water, hoisin sauce, the 1½ teaspoons sesame seeds, ginger, chili sauce, and garlic. Bring to boiling over medium heat, stirring frequently. Reduce heat. Simmer, covered, for 3 minutes.

2. For a charcoal or gas grill, grill chicken on the rack of a covered grill directly over medium heat for 12 to 15 minutes or until chicken is no longer pink (170°F for breasts; 180°F for thighs), turning once and brushing with some of the sauce during the last 5 minutes of grilling.

3. Reheat the remaining sauce until boiling. Slice chicken. If desired, serve chicken on hot cooked noodles. Spoon the remaining sauce over chicken. If desired, sprinkle with additional sesame seeds and garnish with green onion curls.
MAKES 6 SERVINGS

***Tip:** To toast sesame seeds, scatter them in a small dry skillet and heat over medium heat just until golden. Stir frequently to prevent seeds from burning.

Mediterranean Chicken and Polenta

PREP: 20 minutes
BAKE: 10 minutes
OVEN: 375°F

NUTRITION FACTS PER SERVING

Calories 370
Fat 8 g
Cholesterol 66 mg
Sodium 575 mg
Carbohydrates 46 g
Fiber 3 g
Protein 30 g

½ 6.5-ounce jar oil-packed dried tomatoes with Italian herbs
4 small skinless, boneless chicken breast halves (1 to 1¼ pounds total)
   Salt
   Ground black pepper
1 cup assorted olives, drained
½ cup dry white wine or reduced-sodium chicken broth
4 small bay leaves (optional)
3 cups water
1 cup cornmeal
1 cup cold water
1 teaspoon salt

1. Preheat oven to 375°F. Drain tomatoes, reserving the oil. Season chicken with salt and pepper. In a large oven-going skillet heat the reserved oil over medium-high heat. Cook chicken in hot oil about 6 minutes or until browned, turning once. Add tomatoes, olives, wine, and, if desired, bay leaves. Place skillet in oven. Bake, uncovered, for 10 to 15 minutes or until chicken is tender and no longer pink (170°F).

2. Meanwhile, for polenta, in a large saucepan bring the 3 cups water to boiling. In a medium bowl combine cornmeal, the 1 cup cold water, and the 1 teaspoon salt; gradually stir into boiling water. Cook and stir until thickened and bubbly. Reduce heat; stir occasionally.

3. Remove chicken from oven; discard bay leaves (if using). Serve chicken and olives with polenta.
MAKES 4 SERVINGS

Jerk Chicken and Slaw

START TO FINISH: **20 minutes**

NUTRITION FACTS
PER SERVING

Calories 205
Fat 2 g
Cholesterol 66 mg
Sodium 318 mg
Carbohydrates 19 g
Fiber 3 g
Protein 29 g

3   heads baby bok choy, trimmed and thinly sliced
2   cups shredded red cabbage
½   of a peeled, cored fresh pineapple, chopped
2   tablespoons cider vinegar
4   teaspoons packed brown sugar
2   teaspoons all-purpose flour
2   teaspoons jerk seasoning
    Nonstick cooking spray
4   small skinless, boneless chicken breast halves

1. For slaw, in an extra-large bowl combine bok choy, cabbage, and pineapple. Combine vinegar and 2 teaspoons of the brown sugar. Drizzle over slaw; toss to coat. Set aside.

2. In a large resealable plastic bag combine the remaining 2 teaspoons of the brown sugar, the flour, and jerk seasoning. Add chicken; shake well to coat. Lightly coat an extra-large nonstick skillet or grill pan with cooking spray; heat over medium heat. Add chicken to hot skillet. Cook for 6 to 8 minutes, turning once, until no pink remains (170°F). Remove chicken to cutting board.

3. Slice chicken. Serve chicken with slaw. **MAKES 4 SERVINGS**

Spa Chicken

PREP: 30 minutes   COOK: 20 minutes

4   small skinless, boneless chicken breast halves (about 1¼ pounds)
    Salt and ground black pepper
1   tablespoon butter or olive oil
2   cups mushrooms, such as cremini, baby portobello, or button mushrooms, sliced
2   cups sliced leeks
2   tablespoons finely chopped shallot
¾   cup reduced-sodium chicken broth
2   tablespoons Worcestershire-style marinade for chicken
1   9-ounce package frozen artichoke hearts, thawed
2   tablespoons fat-free sour cream
4   teaspoons all-purpose flour
1   tablespoon Dijon mustard
½   cup chopped roma tomatoes
2   tablespoons snipped fresh Italian (flat-leaf) parsley (optional)

1. Season chicken with salt and pepper. In a large nonstick skillet brown chicken in hot butter over medium heat for 2 minutes on each side. Remove from skillet. Cover to keep warm. Add mushrooms, leeks, and shallot to skillet. Cook and stir until mushrooms are tender. Return chicken to skillet; add ½ cup of the broth, Worcestershire-style marinade, and artichoke hearts. Bring to boiling; reduce heat. Simmer, covered, 10 minutes or until no pink remains in chicken (170°F).

2. Meanwhile for sauce, in a bowl combine sour cream, flour, mustard, and remaining ¼ cup chicken broth. Remove chicken and vegetables to serving platter with a slotted spoon; cover and keep warm. Stir sauce into skillet; cook and stir until thickened and bubbly. Cook and stir 1 minute more. Spoon sauce over chicken. Sprinkle with tomatoes and, if desired, parsley. **MAKES 4 SERVINGS**

Ginger Chicken Kabobs

PREP: 25 minutes
CHILL: 2 hours
GRILL: 8 minutes

NUTRITION FACTS
PER SERVING

Calories 175
Fat 3 g
Cholesterol 66 mg
Sodium 212 mg
Carbohydrates 8 g
Fiber 1 g
Protein 27 g

1 pound skinless, boneless chicken breast halves, cut into 1-inch pieces
2 tablespoons finely snipped fresh cilantro
1 tablespoon grated fresh ginger
2 cloves garlic, minced
1 fresh serrano chile pepper, seeded and finely chopped (see tip, page 114)
1 teaspoon cooking oil
½ teaspoon ground coriander
½ teaspoon ground cumin
¼ teaspoon salt
¼ teaspoon garam masala (optional)
⅛ teaspoon ground nutmeg
1 cup fresh pineapple cubes
½ of a medium red sweet pepper, cut into 1-inch pieces
½ of a medium green sweet pepper, cut into 1-inch pieces

1. Place chicken in a large resealable plastic bag set in a shallow dish. Add cilantro, ginger, garlic, serrano pepper, oil, coriander, cumin, salt, garam masala (if desired), and nutmeg to chicken in bag. Seal bag. Turn and press bag to coat chicken. Chill for at least 2 hours or up to 6 hours.

2. On eight 10- to 12-inch skewers, alternately thread the chicken, pineapple, red sweet pepper, and green sweet pepper, leaving a ¼ inch between pieces. (If using wooden skewers, soak in water for 30 minutes before using.)

3. Place kabobs on the rack of an uncovered grill directly over medium coals. Grill for 8 to 10 minutes or until chicken is no longer pink, turning occasionally to brown evenly. **MAKES 4 SERVINGS**

Curry-Lime Chicken Kabobs

PREP: 30 minutes
MARINATE: 4 hours
GRILL: 18 minutes

NUTRITION FACTS
PER SERVING

Calories 263
Fat 9 g
Cholesterol 68 mg
Sodium 336 mg
Carbohydrates 15 g
Fiber 2 g
Protein 30 g

- 1 pound skinless, boneless chicken breast halves, cut into 1½-inch pieces
- 1 6-ounce carton plain yogurt
- ¼ cup snipped fresh cilantro
- 1 teaspoon finely shredded lime peel
- 2 tablespoons lime juice
- 2 tablespoons olive oil or vegetable oil
- 1 tablespoon honey
- 1 tablespoon Dijon mustard
- 2 cloves garlic, minced
- ½ teaspoon curry powder
- ¼ teaspoon salt
- ¼ teaspoon black pepper
- 2 green and/or red sweet peppers, cut into 1-inch pieces
- 1 zucchini, cut into ½-inch slices
- 8 yellow or red cherry tomatoes

1. Place chicken in a resealable plastic bag set in a large bowl. For marinade, in a small bowl combine yogurt, cilantro, lime peel, lime juice, oil, honey, mustard, garlic, curry powder, salt, and black pepper. Pour marinade over chicken. Seal bag; turn to coat chicken. Marinate in the refrigerator for 4 to 24 hours, turning bag occasionally. Drain chicken, reserving marinade.

2. On 8 skewers, alternately thread chicken, sweet peppers, and zucchini, leaving ¼ inch between pieces. Brush vegetables with reserved marinade. (If using wooden skewers, soak in water for 30 minutes before using.)

3. For a charcoal grill, arrange medium-hot coals around a drip pan. Test for medium heat above pan. Place chicken kabobs on grill rack over drip pan. Cover and grill for 18 to 20 minutes or until chicken is no longer pink, turning once halfway through grilling and threading a tomato onto each skewer during the last 1 minute of grilling. (For a gas grill, preheat grill. Reduce heat to medium. Adjust for indirect cooking. Grill as above.)

MAKES 4 SERVINGS

Grilled Chicken and Creamy Corn

PREP: 15 minutes
GRILL: 12 minutes

NUTRITION FACTS PER SERVING

Calories 267   *Fat* 11 g   *Cholesterol* 71 mg   *Sodium* 228 mg   *Carbohydrates* 15 g   *Fiber* 2 g   *Protein* 29 g

2   tablespoons olive oil
1   teaspoon smoked paprika
3   fresh ears corn, husks and silks removed
4   skinless, boneless chicken breast halves (1 to 1¼ pounds total)
¼   teaspoon salt
⅛   teaspoon ground black pepper
⅓   cup light sour cream
    Fat-free milk
¼   cup shredded fresh basil

1. In small bowl combine olive oil and paprika. Brush corn and chicken with oil mixture. Sprinkle with salt and pepper. For a charcoal or gas grill, place corn and chicken on rack directly over medium heat. Grill, covered, for 12 to 15 minutes or until chicken is no longer pink (170°F), turning once.

2. On a cutting board, place an ear of corn, pointed tip down. While holding each corn cob firmly at stem end to keep in place, use a sharp knife to cut corn from cob, leaving some corn in planks and rotating cob to cut corn. (Use a kitchen towel to grip if necessary.) Transfer corn to a medium bowl; stir in sour cream. Stir in milk to desired creaminess. Slice chicken breasts. Serve with creamy corn and sprinkle with shredded basil.

MAKES 4 SERVINGS

Lemon and Herb Sauced Chicken

PREP: 15 minutes
GRILL: 12 minutes

NUTRITION FACTS
PER SERVING

Calories 281
Fat 12 g
Cholesterol 82 mg
Sodium 376 mg
Carbohydrates 8 g
Fiber 3 g
Protein 35 g

4   skinless, boneless chicken breast halves (1 to 1¼ pounds total)
3   tablespoons canola oil
½   teaspoon salt
¼   teaspoon ground black pepper
12   ounces fresh young green beans
1   tablespoon water
¾   cup fresh Italian (flat-leaf) parsley
1   tablespoon cider vinegar
2   cloves garlic, halved
¼   teaspoon crushed red pepper
1   lemon

1. Brush chicken with 1 tablespoon of the oil; sprinkle with ¼ teaspoon of the salt and the black pepper. For a charcoal or gas grill, place chicken on the rack of a grill directly over medium heat. Grill, covered, for 12 to 15 minutes or until no longer pink (170°F), turning once.

2. Meanwhile, in a 1½-quart microwave-safe baking dish combine green beans and water. Cover loosely with plastic wrap. Microwave on 100 percent power (high) for 3 minutes; drain.

3. For herb sauce, in a small food processor combine parsley, the remaining 2 tablespoons oil, the vinegar, garlic, the remaining ¼ teaspoon salt, and the crushed red pepper. Cover and process until nearly smooth. Finely shred peel from the lemon. Cut lemon in half. Serve chicken and green beans with herb sauce. Garnish with lemon peel. Squeeze lemon juice over all. **MAKES 4 SERVINGS**

Chipotle Chile Chicken with Blueberry Pepper Salsa

PREP: 15 minutes
BAKE: 15 minutes
OVEN: 400°F

NUTRITION FACTS PER SERVING

Calories 279
Fat 5 g
Cholesterol 90 mg
Sodium 420 mg
Carbohydrates 25 g
Fiber 2 g
Protein 34 g

	Nonstick cooking spray
2	tablespoons honey
1	tablespoon butter, melted
2	teaspoons finely chopped canned chipotle chile pepper in adobo sauce (see tip, page 114)
1	teaspoon dried oregano, crushed
½	teaspoon salt
4	small skinless, boneless chicken breast halves (1 to 1¼ pounds total)
1½	cups frozen blueberries, thawed and drained
1	11-ounce can mandarin orange sections, drained
3	tablespoons finely chopped red onion
1	teaspoon finely shredded lime peel
2	teaspoons lime juice

1. Preheat oven to 400°F. Coat a 13×9×2-inch baking pan with cooking spray; set aside.

2. In a small bowl stir together 1 tablespoon of the honey, the melted butter, 1 teaspoon of the chipotle chile, the oregano, and salt. Brush both sides of each chicken breast half with the honey mixture. Arrange chicken in prepared pan. Bake for 15 to 20 minutes or until tender and no longer pink (170°F).

3. Meanwhile, for blueberry pepper salsa, in a medium bowl combine blueberries, orange sections, red onion, lime peel, lime juice, the remaining 1 tablespoon honey, and the remaining 1 teaspoon chipotle chile. Spoon salsa over chicken.
MAKES 4 SERVINGS

Moroccan Meat Loaf

PREP: 10 minutes
BAKE: 20 minutes
OVEN: 425°F

NUTRITION FACTS PER SERVING

Calories 487   *Fat* 11 g   *Cholesterol* 142 mg   *Sodium* 721 mg   *Carbohydrates* 73 g   *Fiber* 5 g   *Protein* 27 g

1½ cups golden raisins
⅓ cup chopped red onion
    (1 small)
½ cup couscous
1   teaspoon salt
1   teaspoon curry powder
1   teaspoon ground cinnamon
¾ cup boiling water
1   pound uncooked ground
    turkey
1   egg, lightly beaten
2   cups grape tomatoes
¼ cup water

1. Preheat oven to 425°F. Position oven rack in upper third of oven. Line an 8×8×2-inch baking pan with foil, extending foil beyond edge of pan; grease foil. Set pan aside. In a large mixing bowl combine 1 cup of the raisins, half of the red onion, the couscous, salt, curry powder, and ½ teaspoon of the cinnamon. Pour the ¾ cup boiling water over the mixture; cover and let stand for 2 minutes. Add turkey and egg; mix well. Pat meat mixture into the prepared pan.

2. Bake meat loaf in the upper third of the oven about 20 minutes or until done (165°F).

3. Meanwhile, for tomato chutney, in a medium saucepan combine the remaining ½ cup raisins, red onion, ½ teaspoon cinnamon, the tomatoes, and the ¼ cup water. Cook, covered, over medium-high heat until tomatoes pop, stirring occasionally. Cover and keep warm.

4. Lift meat loaf from pan with foil. Slice meat loaf and serve with tomato chutney. **MAKES 4 SERVINGS**

Parmesan-Crusted Turkey with Mashed Cauliflower

START TO FINISH: 25 minutes

NUTRITION FACTS PER SERVING

Calories 310
Fat 15 g
Cholesterol 97 mg
Sodium 574 mg
Carbohydrates 10 g
Fiber 2 g
Protein 33 g

3 cups cauliflower (½ of a medium head)
¼ cup water
2 8-ounce turkey breast tenderloins, halved horizontally
  Salt
  Ground black pepper
⅓ cup light mayonnaise
⅓ cup finely shredded Parmesan cheese
3 tablespoons fine dry bread crumbs
2 tablespoons butter
  Snipped fresh Italian (flat-leaf) parsley and/or paprika (optional)

1. Preheat broiler. In a microwave-safe 1½-quart casserole combine cauliflower and the water. Cover and microwave on 100 percent power (high) for 12 to 15 minutes or until very tender, stirring once.

2. Lightly sprinkle halved turkey tenderloins with salt and pepper. Place on the unheated rack of a broiler pan. Broil 4 to 5 inches from heat for 5 minutes. Turn turkey steaks over; broil for 4 minutes more.

3. Meanwhile, in a small bowl stir together mayonnaise, ¼ cup of the Parmesan cheese, and the bread crumbs. Spread over turkey. Broil for 2 to 3 minutes more or until topping is golden and turkey is no longer pink (170°F).

4. Add butter and the remaining Parmesan cheese to cauliflower; mash until smooth. If desired, sprinkle with parsley and/or paprika. Serve immediately with turkey. **MAKES 4 SERVINGS**

Turkey Steaks with Spinach, Pears, and Blue Cheese

START TO FINISH: 20 minutes

NUTRITION FACTS PER SERVING

Calories 240
Fat 9 g
Cholesterol 92 mg
Sodium 380 mg
Carbohydrates 8 g
Fiber 2 g
Protein 31 g

2   turkey breast tenderloins (1 to 1¼ pounds total)
1   teaspoon dried sage, crushed
    Salt
    Freshly ground black pepper
2   tablespoons butter
1   6-ounce package fresh baby spinach
1   large pear, cored and thinly sliced
¼   cup crumbled blue cheese (1 ounce)

1. Horizontally split turkey tenderloins to make four ½-inch-thick steaks. Rub turkey with sage; sprinkle with salt and pepper.

2. In an extra-large skillet melt 1 tablespoon of the butter over medium-high heat. Add turkey steaks; cook for 14 to 16 minutes or until no longer pink (170°F), turning once. (Reduce heat to medium if turkey browns too quickly.) Remove turkey from skillet; cover to keep warm. Add spinach to skillet. Cook and stir just until wilted.

3. Meanwhile, in a small skillet melt the remaining 1 tablespoon butter over medium heat. Add pear slices; cook about 5 minutes or until tender and lightly browned, stirring occasionally.

4. Serve turkey with spinach and pears. Sprinkle with blue cheese.
MAKES 4 SERVINGS

Turkey-Vegetable Casseroles

PREP: 15 minutes
BAKE: 10 minutes
OVEN: 450°F

NUTRITION FACTS PER SERVING

Calories 297
Fat 12 g
Cholesterol 71 mg
Sodium 753 mg
Carbohydrates 23 g
Fiber 3 g
Protein 24 g

1   16-ounce bag frozen stew vegetables (potatoes, carrots, onion, and celery)
1   18-ounce jar home-style gravy (1¾ cups)
1   teaspoon finely snipped fresh sage or ½ teaspoon ground sage
2   cups cut-up cooked turkey or chicken
1   medium cooking apple, thinly sliced in rounds
    Fresh sage leaves (optional)
2   tablespoons butter, melted
¼   teaspoon ground nutmeg
¼   teaspoon ground black pepper

1. Preheat oven to 450°F. In a large microwave-safe bowl combine vegetables, gravy, and the 1 teaspoon sage. Cover with vented plastic wrap. Microwave on 100 percent power (high) for 5 minutes. Add turkey; cover and microwave for 4 to 6 minutes more or until heated through and vegetables are tender, stirring occasionally.

2. Spoon turkey-vegetable mixture into four 14- to 16-ounce casseroles. Top with apple slices and, if desired, fresh sage leaves. Drizzle with melted butter. Evenly sprinkle nutmeg and pepper among the four casseroles.

3. Bake, uncovered, about 10 minutes or until bubbly and apple slices begin to brown.
MAKES 4 SERVINGS

CHAPTER 7

Fish

Parmesan-Crusted Cod

PREP: 15 minutes
BAKE: 4 minutes per ½-inch thickness
OVEN: 450°F

NUTRITION FACTS PER SERVING

Calories 233
Fat 6 g
Cholesterol 84 mg
Sodium 407 mg
Carbohydrates 11 g
Fiber 2 g
Protein 34 g

4   fresh or frozen skinless cod
    fillets (1½ pounds total)
    Nonstick cooking spray
¼   teaspoon salt
⅛   teaspoon ground black pepper
⅓   cup panko bread crumbs
¼   cup finely shredded Parmesan
    cheese
½   cup water
1   10-ounce package julienned
    or shredded fresh carrots
    (3 cups)
1   tablespoon butter
¾   teaspoon ground ginger
    Mixed fresh salad greens
    (optional)

1. Thaw fish, if frozen. Preheat oven to 450°F. Lightly coat a baking sheet with cooking spray. Rinse fish; pat dry with paper towels. Arrange fish on the baking sheet. Sprinkle fish with the salt and pepper. In a small bowl stir together panko and cheese; sprinkle over fish.

2. Bake, uncovered, for 4 to 6 minutes per ½-inch thickness of fish or until crumbs are golden brown and fish flakes easily when tested with a fork.

3. Meanwhile, in a large skillet bring the water to boiling; add carrots. Reduce heat. Cook, covered, over medium heat for 5 minutes. Uncover and cook about 2 minutes more or until water evaporates. Add butter and ginger; toss until butter is melted and carrots are coated. Serve fish with carrots and, if desired, salad greens. **MAKES 4 SERVINGS**

Fish Tostadas with Chili-Lime Cream

START TO FINISH: 20 minutes

NUTRITION FACTS PER SERVING

Calories 278
Fat 14 g
Cholesterol 67 mg
Sodium 303 mg
Carbohydrates 17 g
Fiber 2 g
Protein 25 g

1 pound fresh or frozen tilapia or cod fillets
½ teaspoon chili powder
¼ teaspoon salt
1 lime, halved
½ cup sour cream
½ teaspoon garlic powder
8 6-inch tostada shells
2 cups shredded cabbage mix
1 avocado, halved, seeded, peeled, and sliced (optional)
1 cup cherry tomatoes, quartered
Bottled hot pepper sauce (optional)

1. Thaw fish, if frozen. Rinse fish; pat dry with paper towels. Sprinkle fish with ¼ teaspoon of the chili powder and the salt; set aside. Preheat broiler. For chili-lime cream, in a small bowl squeeze 2 teaspoons juice from half the lime. Stir in sour cream, garlic powder, and the remaining ¼ teaspoon chili powder; set aside. Cut the remaining lime half into wedges for serving.

2. Place fish on the unheated greased rack of a broiler pan; tuck under thin edges to make fish an even thickness. Measure thickness. Place tostada shells on baking sheet. Place in oven on the lowest rack. Broil fish 4 inches from heat for 4 to 6 minutes per ½-inch thickness or until fish flakes easily when tested with a fork. Break fish into chunks. Top tostada shells with fish, chili-lime cream, cabbage mix, avocado (if using), tomatoes, and, if desired, hot pepper sauce. Serve with lime wedges.

MAKES 4 SERVINGS

Grilled Cod with Red Pepper Sauce

PREP: 30 minutes
GRILL: 4 minutes per ½-inch thickness

4   4-ounce fresh or frozen skinless cod fillets
1   tablespoon olive oil
1¼ cups chopped red sweet pepper (1 large)
1   cup chopped, seeded, peeled tomatoes (2 medium)
2   tablespoons white wine vinegar
¼   teaspoon salt
    Dash cayenne pepper
1   tablespoon olive oil
1   tablespoon snipped fresh basil or oregano or ½ teaspoon dried basil or oregano, crushed
    Red and/or yellow cherry tomatoes (optional)
    Fresh basil or oregano sprigs (optional)

1. Thaw fish, if frozen. Rinse fish; pat dry with paper towels. Measure thickness of fish; set aside.

2. For red pepper sauce, in a small skillet heat 1 tablespoon oil over medium heat. Add sweet pepper; cook for 3 to 5 minutes or until tender, stirring occasionally. Stir in chopped tomatoes, 1 tablespoon of the vinegar, the salt, and cayenne pepper. Cook about 5 minutes or until tomatoes are softened, stirring occasionally. Cool slightly. Transfer mixture to a food processor or blender. Cover and process or blend until smooth. Return sauce to skillet; cover and keep warm.

3. In a small bowl stir together the remaining 1 tablespoon vinegar, 1 tablespoon oil, and snipped basil; brush over both sides of fish. Place fish in a greased grill basket, tucking under any thin edges.

4. For a charcoal or gas grill, grill fish in basket on the rack of a covered grill directly over medium heat until fish flakes easily when tested with a fork, turning basket once. Allow 4 to 6 minutes per ½-inch thickness of fish.

5. Serve fish with red pepper sauce. If desired, serve with cherry tomatoes and fresh basil sprigs.
MAKES 4 SERVINGS

Catfish 'n' Chips

PREP: 15 minutes
BAKE: 10 minutes
OVEN: 450°F

NUTRITION FACTS
PER SERVING

Calories 317
Fat 13 g
Cholesterol 54 mg
Sodium 449 mg
Carbohydrates 28 g
Fiber 3 g
Protein 22 g

1 pound fresh or frozen skinless catfish fillets
  Nonstick cooking spray
1 teaspoon chili powder or paprika
½ teaspoon salt
¼ teaspoon dried dill
¼ teaspoon ground black pepper
2 small sweet potatoes (10 ounces)
1 medium Yukon gold potato
1 tablespoon canola oil
⅓ cup buttermilk
⅔ cup panko bread crumbs
2 cloves garlic, minced
  Fresh dill sprigs (optional)
  Malt vinegar (optional)

1. Thaw fish, if frozen. Rinse fish; pat dry with paper towels. Cut fish into four to eight serving-size pieces. Set fish aside. Preheat oven to 450°F. Line two baking sheets with foil; lightly coat with cooking spray. For seasoning, in a small bowl combine chili powder, salt, dill, and pepper; set aside.

2. Scrub sweet and Yukon gold potatoes. Cut potatoes into ½-inch thick wedges and place in a large bowl. Drizzle potatoes with oil and sprinkle ½ teaspoon of the seasoning; toss to coat. Arrange potatoes in a single layer on one prepared baking sheet. Bake for 10 minutes.

3. Meanwhile, pour buttermilk in a shallow dish. In another shallow dish combine panko, garlic, and the remaining seasoning. Dip fish in buttermilk, turning to coat and allowing excess to drip off. Dip in panko mixture, coating both sides. Place fish on second baking sheet. Lightly coat with cooking spray. Measure thickness of fish.

4. Bake for 4 to 6 minutes per ½-inch thickness of fish or until fish flakes easily when tested with a fork and potatoes are tender. If desired, sprinkle fish with fresh dill and serve with malt vinegar.
MAKES 4 SERVINGS

Lemon-Ginger Fish

START TO FINISH: 20 minutes

NUTRITION FACTS PER SERVING

Calories 228
Fat 12 g
Cholesterol 79 mg
Sodium 344 mg
Carbohydrates 9 g
Fiber 3 g
Protein 22 g

1   pound fresh or frozen cod or other firm white fish fillets
2   small lemons
1   tablespoon grated fresh ginger
2   teaspoons sugar
¼   cup butter
2   5-ounce packages fresh baby spinach
2   tablespoons water
¼   teaspoon salt
¼   teaspoon ground black pepper

1. Thaw fish, if frozen. Rinse fish; pat dry with paper towels. Cut fish into 4 pieces; set fish aside. Thinly slice one lemon; set aside. Finely shred peel from the remaining lemon; juice the lemon. In a small bowl combine the lemon peel and juice, ginger, and sugar. Set aside.

2. In a large skillet melt butter over medium heat. Add fish to skillet. Cook for 1 to 2 minutes or until browned. Turn fish; add lemon juice mixture to skillet. Cover and cook for 2 to 3 minutes or until fish flakes when tested with a fork. Using a slotted spatula, transfer fish to platter; cover to keep warm.

3. Add lemon slices to the skillet. Cook about 2 minutes or until lemon slices are softened and liquid is slightly thickened.

4. Meanwhile, place spinach in an extra-large microwave-safe bowl. Sprinkle with the water. Microwave on 100 percent power (high) about 2 minutes or just until wilted, tossing once after 1 minute.

5. To serve, divide spinach among four shallow serving bowls. Top with fish. Spoon lemon slices and cooking liquid over fish and spinach. Sprinkle with salt and pepper. **MAKES 4 SERVINGS**

Orange-Pepper Salmon:
Prepare as directed, except substitute salmon for the cod and 2 small oranges for the lemons. Omit ginger; add ¼ teaspoon crushed red pepper to the juice mixture.

Peanut-Crusted Salmon

PREP: 20 minutes
BAKE: 8 minutes
OVEN: 450°F

NUTRITION FACTS PER SERVING

Calories 356   *Fat* 18 g   *Cholesterol* 78 mg   *Sodium* 177 mg   *Carbohydrates* 13 g   *Fiber* 2 g   *Protein* 32 g

6   5- to 6-ounce fresh or frozen skinless salmon fillets, about 1 inch thick
2   to 3 tablespoons orange juice
¼   teaspoon salt
⅛   teaspoon coarse ground black pepper
1   cup whole wheat panko bread crumbs
⅓   cup peanuts, toasted and finely chopped (see tip, page 15)
2   tablespoons finely snipped fresh parsley
2   tablespoons olive oil
2   cloves garlic, minced
2   teaspoons finely shredded orange peel
½   cup dry white wine or chicken broth

1. Preheat oven to 450°F. Thaw fish, if frozen. Rinse fish; pat dry with paper towels. Drizzle fish with orange juice. Sprinkle with salt and pepper.

2. In a shallow dish combine panko, chopped peanuts, parsley, oil, garlic, and orange peel. Dip fish into peanut mixture, turning and pressing to coat.

3. Place fish in a single layer in an ungreased 3-quart rectangular baking dish. Pour wine into dish. Bake, uncovered, for 8 to 12 minutes or until fish flakes easily when tested with a fork. **MAKES 6 SERVINGS**

Salmon with Cilantro-Pineapple Salsa

PREP: 20 minutes
GRILL: 8 minutes

NUTRITION FACTS PER SERVING

Calories 257
Fat 12 g
Cholesterol 66 mg
Sodium 219 mg
Carbohydrates 13 g
Fiber 2 g
Protein 23 g

1 pound fresh or frozen skinless salmon fillet, about 1 inch thick
2 cups coarsely chopped fresh pineapple
½ cup chopped red or green sweet pepper
¼ cup finely chopped red onion
½ teaspoon finely shredded lime peel (set aside)
3 tablespoons lime juice
1 fresh jalapeño pepper, seeded and finely chopped (see tip, page 114)
2 tablespoons snipped fresh cilantro or parsley
½ teaspoon chili powder
¼ teaspoon salt
   Dash cayenne pepper
   Lime wedges (optional)
   Torn lettuce (optional)

1. Thaw fish, if frozen. Rinse fish; pat dry with paper towels. For salsa, in a medium bowl combine chopped pineapple, sweet pepper, red onion, 2 tablespoons of the lime juice, the jalapeño, and 1 tablespoon of the cilantro. Set aside. In a small bowl combine lime peel, the remaining 1 tablespoon lime juice, the remaining 1 tablespoon cilantro, the chili powder, salt, and cayenne pepper. Brush on both sides of fish.

2. Grease a wire grill basket. Place fish in grill basket, tucking under any thin edges for an even thickness. Place fish in grill basket on the rack of an uncovered grill directly over medium coals. Grill for 8 to 12 minutes or just until fish flakes easily with a fork, carefully turning once halfway through grilling.

3. To serve, cut fish into 4 serving-size pieces; top with salsa. If desired, serve with lime wedges and lettuce. **MAKES 4 SERVINGS**

Salmon and Spring Vegetables with Dill

START TO FINISH: **20 minutes**

NUTRITION FACTS
PER SERVING

Calories 328
Fat 15 g
Cholesterol 67 mg
Sodium 365 mg
Carbohydrates 23 g
Fiber 4 g
Protein 28 g

2   4-ounce fresh or frozen skinless salmon fillets
10 ounces fresh asparagus spears, trimmed
6   ounces tiny new potatoes, cut into 1-inch pieces
2   tablespoons white or dark balsamic vinegar
1   teaspoon cooking oil
1   teaspoon snipped fresh dill or ½ teaspoon dried dill
¼   teaspoon salt
⅛   teaspoon ground black pepper
Fresh dill (optional)

1. Thaw salmon, if frozen. Rinse salmon; pat dry with paper towels. Arrange salmon in a microwave-safe 2-quart square baking dish. Arrange asparagus and potatoes around salmon. In a small bowl combine balsamic vinegar, oil, snipped or dried dill, salt, and pepper. Drizzle over salmon and vegetables.

2. Cover with vented plastic wrap. Cook on 100 percent power (high) for 10 to 12 minutes or until fish flakes easily when tested with a fork and vegetables are tender, turning dish once halfway through cooking if necessary. If desired, garnish servings with additional fresh dill. **MAKES 2 SERVINGS**

Steamed Orange Salmon

PREP: 15 minutes   COOK: 6 minutes

4   4- to 5-ounce fresh or frozen skinless salmon fillets
1   orange
2   teaspoons olive oil
1   teaspoon toasted sesame seeds
¼   teaspoon salt
¼   teaspoon ground white pepper
     Orange slices and/or toasted sesame seeds (see tip, page 92) (optional)

1. Thaw fish, if frozen. Rinse fish; pat dry with paper towels; set aside. Finely shred 2 teaspoons peel from the orange; set aside. Thinly slice orange and lay slices evenly in a steamer basket. Place the fish in a single layer on the orange slices. In a small bowl combine orange peel, olive oil, 1 teaspoon sesame seeds, the salt, and pepper. Spoon evenly over salmon fillets.

2. Fill a large Dutch oven* with water to a depth of 1 inch. Bring water to boiling. Carefully place steamer basket over water. Cover and steam over gently boiling water for 6 to 8 minutes or until fish flakes easily when tested with a fork.

3. To serve, arrange salmon on a serving platter. Discard orange slices. If desired, serve with fresh orange slices and/or sprinkle with additional sesame seeds.
MAKES 4 SERVINGS

*Tip:** Use a Dutch oven large enough to allow the steamer basket to stand fully open so there is enough room for the fish to lie flat.

Shrimp and Tomatoes with Lemon-Caper Sauce

START TO FINISH: 30 minutes

NUTRITION FACTS PER SERVING

Calories 244
Fat 12 g
Cholesterol 172 mg
Sodium 239 mg
Carbohydrates 10 g
Fiber 4 g
Protein 25 g

1⅓ pounds fresh or frozen medium shrimp in shells
3 tablespoons olive oil
8 ounces fresh French string beans (haricots verts) or other small, thin green beans, trimmed
3 medium tomatoes, cut into wedges
1 teaspoon finely shredded lemon peel
3 tablespoons lemon juice
1 tablespoon capers, drained
2 cups hot cooked pasta (optional)

1. Thaw shrimp, if frozen. Peel and devein shrimp, leaving tails intact if desired. Rinse shrimp; pat dry with paper towels. Set aside.

2. In an extra-large skillet heat 1 tablespoon of the olive oil over medium-high heat. Add green beans to skillet; cook and stir for 3 minutes. Add shrimp; cook and stir about 3 minutes or until shrimp are opaque. Add tomatoes; cook for 1 minute more.

3. For lemon-caper sauce, in a small bowl whisk together the remaining 2 tablespoons olive oil, the lemon peel, lemon juice, and capers.

4. If desired, serve shrimp and tomatoes over hot cooked pasta. Drizzle sauce over all.
MAKES 4 SERVINGS

Stir-Fried Shrimp with Snow Peas

START TO FINISH: 25 minutes

NUTRITION FACTS PER SERVING

Calories 237
Fat 5 g
Cholesterol 108 mg
Sodium 744 mg
Carbohydrates 30 g
Fiber 3 g
Protein 16 g

12   ounces fresh or frozen medium shrimp in shells
1   tablespoon minced fresh ginger
2   teaspoons sherry or rice wine
2   teaspoons cornstarch
⅛   to ¼ teaspoon crushed red pepper (optional)
1   tablespoon canola oil
1   walnut-size piece fresh ginger, crushed*
1   large clove garlic, crushed*
6   ounces fresh snow peas, strings removed**
3   green onions, cut into 1-inch pieces
½   of a small onion, sliced
½   cup chicken broth
2   cups hot cooked brown rice

1. Thaw shrimp, if frozen. Peel and devein shrimp. Rinse shrimp; pat dry with paper towels. Place shrimp in a large bowl. In a small bowl stir together the 1 tablespoon minced ginger, the sherry, cornstarch, and, if desired, crushed red pepper.

2. In a wok or large skillet heat oil over medium-high heat. Add the crushed ginger and garlic; cook for 1 minute. Add snow peas, green onions, and the sliced onion. Cook and stir about 2 minutes or until the snow peas turn bright green. Add the shrimp and broth. Cook and stir for 1 to 2 minutes or until the shrimp are opaque. Serve with brown rice. **MAKES 4 SERVINGS**

*Tip: Crushing ginger and garlic releases aromatic oils and lends mellow richness to the dish. To crush, use the flat side of a knife.

**Tip: Sugar snap peas, Chinese long beans, or Chinese broccoli can be used in place of the snow peas.

Red Cumin-Lime Shrimp on Jicama Rice

START TO FINISH: 30 minutes

NUTRITION FACTS PER SERVING

Calories 284   *Fat* 11 g   *Cholesterol* 129 mg   *Sodium* 350 mg   *Carbohydrates* 26 g   *Fiber* 6 g   *Protein* 21 g

12 ounces fresh or frozen peeled and deveined medium shrimp
3   teaspoons olive oil
1½ cups chopped onions (3 medium)
1   medium fresh Anaheim chile pepper, seeded and sliced (see tip, page 114)
1½ tablespoons chili powder
1½ teaspoons ground cumin
1   cup hot cooked brown rice
1½ cups peeled jicama cut into thin bite-size strips
2   tablespoons lime juice
2   tablespoons 60 to 70 percent vegetable oil spread
¼   teaspoon salt
⅓   cup snipped fresh cilantro
    Lime wedges (optional)

1. Thaw shrimp, if frozen. Rinse shrimp; pat dry with paper towels. Set shrimp aside. In a large nonstick skillet heat 1 teaspoon of the oil over medium-high heat. Tilt and swirl skillet to lightly coat bottom. Add onions and chile pepper; cook about 3 minutes or until tender, stirring frequently. Stir in shrimp, chili powder, and cumin; cook for 3 to 4 minutes or until shrimp are opaque.

2. Meanwhile, spoon the hot rice into a serving bowl. Stir jicama into rice. Cover and let stand until ready to serve.

3. Remove skillet from heat; stir in the remaining 2 teaspoons oil, the lime juice, vegetable oil spread, and salt. Cover and let stand for 5 minutes to allow the flavors to absorb and the vegetable oil spread to melt.

4. Stir cilantro into jicama rice. Serve shrimp mixture over jicama rice. If desired, pass lime wedges.
MAKES 4 SERVINGS

Greek Leeks and Shrimp Stir-Fry

START TO FINISH: 30 minutes

NUTRITION FACTS PER SERVING

Calories 433
Fat 10 g
Cholesterol 232 mg
Sodium 548 mg
Carbohydrates 45 g
Fiber 3 g
Protein 38 g

1¼ pounds fresh or frozen peeled, deveined medium shrimp
⅔ cup water
⅓ cup lemon juice
1 tablespoon cornstarch
¾ teaspoon bouquet garni seasoning or dried oregano, crushed
1 cup quick-cooking couscous
½ teaspoon dried oregano, crushed
¼ teaspoon salt
1½ cups boiling water
1 tablespoon olive oil
1⅓ cups thinly sliced leeks
½ cup crumbled feta cheese (2 ounces)

1. Thaw shrimp, if frozen. Rinse shrimp; pat dry with paper towels. Set shrimp aside.

2. In a small bowl combine the ⅔ cup water, lemon juice, cornstarch, and ¼ teaspoon of the bouquet garni seasoning; set aside.

3. In a small bowl combine couscous, oregano, salt, and the remaining ½ teaspoon bouquet garni seasoning. Pour boiling water over couscous. Cover and let stand for 5 minutes.

4. Meanwhile, in a wok or extra-large skillet heat oil over medium heat. Add leeks; cook and stir for 2 to 3 minutes or until tender. Remove leeks from wok; set aside. Stir lemon juice mixture; add to wok. Bring to boiling. Add shrimp; cook for 2 to 3 minutes or until shrimp are opaque. Stir in cooked leeks and ¼ cup of the feta cheese.

5. To serve, fluff couscous with a fork. Transfer couscous to a serving platter. Spoon shrimp mixture over couscous. Sprinkle with the remaining ¼ cup feta cheese. **MAKES 4 SERVINGS**

Shrimp Fried Rice

START TO FINISH: 30 minutes

NUTRITION FACTS
PER SERVING

Calories 304
Fat 8 g
Cholesterol 182 mg
Sodium 575 mg
Carbohydrates 4 g
Fiber 4 g
Protein 26 g

12 ounces fresh or frozen
    medium shrimp in shells
1   egg
2   egg whites
4   teaspoons canola oil
½   cup chopped carrot
    (1 medium)
½   cup chopped celery (1 stalk)
½   cup sliced fresh mushrooms
½   cup sliced green onions (4)
1   teaspoon grated fresh ginger
2   cups unsalted cooked brown
    rice, chilled
½   of a 14-ounce can bean
    sprouts, rinsed and drained
    (1 cup)
½   cup frozen baby sweet peas
2   tablespoons reduced-sodium
    soy sauce

1. Thaw shrimp, if frozen. Peel and devein shrimp. Rinse shrimp; pat dry with paper towels and set aside. In a small bowl beat together egg and egg whites; set aside. In a large skillet heat 2 teaspoons of the oil over medium-high heat. Add shrimp; stir-fry about 2 minutes or until shrimp are opaque. Remove shrimp; set aside.

2. Add the remaining 2 teaspoons oil to the skillet. Add carrot, celery, mushrooms, green onions, and ginger; stir-fry for 3 to 4 minutes or until vegetables are tender. Add beaten eggs; let stand for 5 to 10 seconds or until egg set on bottom but remain runny on top. Add rice and bean sprouts. Turn and toss mixture continuously for 1 minute. Stir in shrimp, peas, and soy sauce; heat through.
MAKES 4 SERVINGS

Shrimp-Artichoke Frittata

START TO FINISH: 30 minutes

NUTRITION FACTS PER SERVING

Calories 126   *Fat* 3 g   *Cholesterol* 37 mg   *Sodium* 343 mg   *Carbohydrates* 6 g   *Fiber* 2 g   *Protein* 19 g

4   ounces fresh or frozen shrimp
     in shells
½   of a 9-ounce package frozen
     artichoke hearts
2   cups refrigerated or frozen
     egg product, thawed
¼   cup fat-free milk
¼   cup thinly sliced green
     onions (2)
⅛   teaspoon garlic powder
⅛   teaspoon ground black pepper
     Nonstick cooking spray
3   tablespoons finely shredded
     Parmesan cheese
     Snipped fresh parsley

1. Thaw shrimp, if frozen. Peel and devein shrimp. Rinse shrimp; pat dry. Halve shrimp lengthwise; set aside. Meanwhile, cook artichoke hearts according to package directions; drain. Cut artichoke hearts in quarters; set aside.

2. Stir together egg product, milk, 2 tablespoons of the green onions, the garlic powder, and pepper; set aside.

3. Lightly coat a large nonstick skillet with cooking spray. Heat skillet until a drop of water sizzles. Add shrimp to skillet; cook shrimp for 1 to 3 minutes or until shrimp turn opaque.

4. Pour egg mixture into skillet; do not stir. Place skillet over medium-low heat. As the egg mixture sets, run a spatula around the edge of the skillet, lifting edges to allow liquid to run underneath. Continue cooking and lifting edges until mixture is almost set (top will be wet).

5. Remove skillet from heat; sprinkle artichoke pieces evenly over the top. Sprinkle with Parmesan cheese. Let stand, covered, for 3 to 4 minutes or until top is set. Top with the remaining 2 tablespoons green onions and parsley. Loosen edges of frittata. Transfer to a serving plate; cut into wedges to serve. **MAKES 4 SERVINGS**

Cajun Shrimp Stir-Fry in a Grill Wok

PREP: 20 minutes
GRILL: 6 minutes

NUTRITION FACTS PER SERVING

Calories 249
Fat 14 g
Cholesterol 129 mg
Sodium 185 mg
Carbohydrates 13 g
Fiber 4 g
Protein 20 g

12 ounces fresh or frozen peeled and deveined medium shrimp
2 tablespoons canola oil
2 cups red and/or yellow sweet pepper strips (2 medium)
1 cup thin onion wedges
1 cup broccoli florets or zucchini chunks
1 teaspoon Cajun seasoning
   Nonstick cooking spray
¼ cup chopped pecans, toasted*
1 tablespoon snipped fresh parsley
   Lime wedges (optional)

1. Thaw shrimp, if frozen. Rinse shrimp; pat dry with paper towels. In a medium bowl combine shrimp and 1 tablespoon of the oil; toss gently to coat. Set aside.

2. In a large bowl combine sweet pepper strips, onion wedges, broccoli, and the Cajun seasoning. Drizzle with the remaining 1 tablespoon oil; toss vegetables gently to coat.

3. Lightly coat a grill wok with cooking spray. For a charcoal grill, place grill wok on the rack of an uncovered grill directly over medium-hot coals. Heat wok for 5 minutes. Carefully add shrimp; grill for 2 to 3 minutes or until shrimp begin to brown, stirring occasionally. Add vegetable mixture to wok; grill and stir for 4 to 6 minutes or until shrimp are opaque and vegetables are tender. (For a gas grill, preheat grill. Reduce heat to medium-high. Place grill wok on grill rack directly over heat. Cover and heat wok, then grill as above.)

4. Sprinkle Cajun shrimp with toasted pecans and parsley. If desired, serve with lime wedges.
MAKES 4 SERVINGS

*Tip: To toast nuts, spread them in a shallow baking pan. Bake in a 350°F oven for 5 to 10 minutes or until light brown, shaking pan once or twice. Watch carefully to prevent nuts from burning.

CHAPTER 8

Vegetarian

Rigatoni with Broccoli, Beans, and Basil

START TO FINISH: 25 minutes

NUTRITION FACTS PER SERVING

Calories 456
Fat 15 g
Cholesterol 0 mg
Sodium 601 mg
Carbohydrates 70 g
Fiber 9 g
Protein 17 g

8   ounces dried rigatoni (about 3½ cups)
2   cups broccoli florets
1   19-ounce can cannellini beans (white kidney beans), rinsed and drained
2   teaspoons bottled minced garlic
4   tablespoons olive oil
¼   cup snipped fresh basil
½   teaspoon salt
2   slices bread, cut into small cubes
¼   teaspoon crushed red pepper
    Snipped fresh basil (optional)

1. In a large pot cook pasta according to package directions, adding broccoli for the last 5 minutes of cooking. Drain, reserving ¾ cup of the pasta water. Return pasta and broccoli to pot; keep warm.

2. Meanwhile, in a large bowl combine beans, garlic, and 3 tablespoons of the oil. Mash about half of the bean mixture. Stir in basil, salt, and the reserved pasta water. Stir bean mixture into pasta and broccoli in pot. Cover and keep warm.

3. For croutons, in a large skillet heat the remaining 1 tablespoon oil over medium heat. Add bread cubes and crushed red pepper. Cook and stir for 1 to 2 minutes, until crisp. Top pasta with croutons and, if desired, additional basil.
MAKES 4 SERVINGS

Greek Spinach Pasta Salad with Feta and Beans

START TO FINISH: 25 minutes

NUTRITION FACTS PER SERVING

Calories 408
Fat 10 g
Cholesterol 19 mg
Sodium 487 mg
Carbohydrates 62 g
Fiber 6 g
Protein 17 g

12 ounces dried cavatappi or farfalle pasta
1   15-ounce can Great Northern beans, rinsed and drained
1   5- to 6-ounce package fresh baby spinach
1   cup crumbled feta cheese (4 ounces)
¼   cup dried tomatoes (not oil-packed), snipped
¼   cup chopped green onions (2)
1   teaspoon finely shredded lemon peel
2   tablespoons lemon juice
2   tablespoons olive oil
1   tablespoon snipped fresh oregano
1   tablespoon snipped fresh lemon thyme or thyme
½   teaspoon kosher salt or sea salt
½   teaspoon freshly ground black pepper
2   cloves garlic, minced
    Shaved Parmesan or Pecorino Romano cheese (optional)

1. Cook pasta according to package directions.

2. Meanwhile, in a large serving bowl combine beans, spinach, feta cheese, tomatoes, green onions, lemon peel, lemon juice, oil, oregano, thyme, salt, pepper, and garlic.

2. Drain pasta, reserving ¼ cup of the cooking water. Toss pasta and the reserved pasta water with spinach mixture. Serve warm or at room temperature. If desired, top with shaved Parmesan cheese.
MAKES 6 SERVINGS

Tofu Pad Thai

START TO FINISH: **30 minutes**

NUTRITION FACTS PER SERVING

Calories 389   *Fat* 14 g   *Cholesterol* 47 mg   *Sodium* 1,000 mg   *Carbohydrates* 50 g   *Fiber* 4 g   *Protein* 16 g

5   ounces dried brown rice fettuccine
3   tablespoons rice vinegar
3   tablespoons packed brown sugar
2   tablespoons Asian chile bean sauce
2   tablespoons fish sauce or reduced-sodium soy sauce
1   tablespoon tamarind pulp concentrate
3   cloves garlic, minced
    Nonstick cooking spray
1   egg, lightly beaten (optional)
1   tablespoon canola oil
3   cups coarsely shredded napa cabbage
1   cup packaged julienned fresh carrots
4   green onions, cut into 1-inch pieces
½   to 1 fresh Thai chile pepper, cut into thin strips (see tip, page 114)
1   18-ounce package firm, tub-style tofu (fresh bean curd), drained and cut into ½-inch-thick slices
¼   cup unsalted dry-roasted peanuts
2   tablespoons snipped fresh cilantro
1   lime, quartered

1. Cook fettuccine according to package directions, except cook for 2 minutes less than the suggested time; drain. Rinse with cold water; drain again.

2. Meanwhile, for sauce, in a small bowl combine vinegar, brown sugar, chile bean sauce, fish sauce, tamarind, and garlic; set aside.

3. Coat a wok or large nonstick skillet with cooking spray; heat wok over medium heat. Add egg if using. Immediately begin stirring gently but continuously until egg resembles small pieces of cooked egg surrounded by liquid egg. Stop stirring; cook for 20 to 30 seconds or until egg is set. Turn egg over; cook for 20 to 30 seconds more or until egg is cooked through. Transfer egg to a cutting board; set aside.

4. Add 1 teaspoon of the oil to wok; add cabbage, carrots, green onions, and chile pepper. Cook and stir over medium-high heat for 2 to 3 minutes or until vegetables are crisp-tender. Remove vegetables from wok.

5. Add the remaining 2 teaspoons oil to wok; add tofu slices. Cook for 4 to 5 minutes or until tofu is light brown, turning occasionally. Remove tofu from wok. Add sauce and cooked fettuccine. Cook and stir for 2 to 3 minutes or until fettuccine is tender but still firm. Return vegetables and tofu to wok. Cook for 1 to 2 minutes or until heated through, gently stirring occasionally. Cut egg into thin slices; gently stir into pad thai.

6. Divide pad thai among serving plates. Sprinkle with peanuts and cilantro. Serve with lime quarters.
MAKES 4 SERVINGS

Quinoa and Red Bean Burritos

PREP: 15 minutes
BAKE: 12 minutes
OVEN: 350°F

NUTRITION FACTS PER BURRITO

Calories 315
Fat 8 g
Cholesterol 13 mg
Sodium 734 mg
Carbohydrates 47 g
Fiber 8 g
Protein 14 g

1   cup quinoa*
2   cups water
2   teaspoons smoky-sweet pepper blend
1   15-ounce can red kidney beans, rinsed, drained, and slightly mashed
1½ cups purchased salsa
     Nonstick cooking spray
8   7- or 8-inch whole wheat tortillas
1   cup shredded Mexican-style four cheese

1. Rinse quinoa; drain. In a medium saucepan bring water to boiling. Slowly add quinoa and pepper blend to boiling water. Return to boiling; reduce heat. Simmer, covered, about 15 minutes. Drain if necessary. Stir in beans and 1 cup of the salsa.

2. Meanwhile preheat oven to 350°F. Lightly coat a large baking sheet with cooking spray.

3. Wrap tortillas in paper towels. Microwave on 100 percent power (high) for 45 seconds or until softened. Place ½ cup of the quinoa mixture in the center of each tortilla. Fold up bottom edge of tortilla over filling. Fold in opposite sides over filling. Roll up from bottoms. Place on prepared

baking sheet. Lightly coat burritos with cooking spray. Top burritos with the remaining ½ cup salsa and the cheese.

4. Bake burritos about 12 minutes, until heated through and cheese is melted. If desired, serve with additional salsa. **MAKES 8 BURRITOS**

*Tip: Rinsing quinoa before cooking it is an important step. The grain is coated with a naturally occurring substance that has a bitter taste to keep insects from eating it on the plant. Some, but not all, quinoa is rinsed before packaging. Read the labels and to ensure good taste, rinse before cooking.

Mediterranean Edamame Toss

PREP: 20 minutes
COOK: 15 minutes

NUTRITION FACTS
PER SERVING

Calories 236
Fat 12 g
Cholesterol 3 mg
Sodium 276 mg
Carbohydrates 5 g
Fiber 5 g
Protein 11 g

½ cup uncooked quinoa, rinsed and drained
1 cup water
1 cup ready-to-eat fresh or frozen, thawed shelled sweet soybeans (edamame)
2 tomatoes, seeded and chopped
1 cup fresh arugula or spinach leaves
½ cup chopped red onion
2 tablespoons olive oil
1 teaspoon finely shredded lemon peel
2 tablespoons lemon juice
¼ cup reduced-fat feta cheese, crumbled
2 tablespoons snipped fresh basil
¼ teaspoon salt
¼ teaspoon freshly ground black pepper

1. In a medium saucepan combine quinoa and the water. Bring to boiling; reduce heat. Cover and simmer about 15 minutes, until quinoa is tender and liquid is absorbed, adding edamame the last 4 minutes of cooking.

2. In a large bowl combine quinoa mixture, tomatoes, arugula, and onion.

3. In a small bowl whisk together olive oil, lemon peel, and lemon juice. Stir in half the cheese, the basil, salt, and pepper. Add to quinoa mixture, tossing to coat. Sprinkle with remaining cheese. Serve at room temperature.
MAKES 4 SERVINGS

Roasted Vegetables over Rosemary Polenta

PREP: 20 minutes COOK: 5 minutes ROAST: 17 minutes
OVEN: 450°F

NUTRITION FACTS PER SERVING

Calories 278 *Fat* 6 g *Cholesterol* 2 mg *Sodium* 308 mg *Carbohydrates* 47 g *Fiber* 8 g *Protein* 10 g

3 roma tomatoes, quartered
2 medium yellow summer squash and/or zucchini, cut into 1-inch chunks
1 medium red or green sweet pepper, cut into strips
1 medium red onion, cut into thin wedges
1 tablespoon olive oil
½ teaspoon salt
¼ teaspoon cracked black pepper
1 cup frozen shelled sweet soybeans (edamame), thawed
2 tablespoons snipped fresh rosemary
3½ cups water
⅛ teaspoon salt
1 cup quick-cooking polenta
¼ cup shredded Parmesan cheese (1 ounce)

1. Preheat oven to 450°F. Combine tomatoes, summer squash, sweet pepper, and onion in a large roasting pan. Drizzle vegetables with oil and sprinkle with the ½ teaspoon salt and the black pepper. Toss lightly to coat.

2. Roast, uncovered, for 12 minutes. Remove from oven. Gently stir in soybeans and 1 tablespoon of the rosemary; roast, uncovered, 5 minutes more or just until vegetables are tender.

3. Meanwhile, in a medium saucepan bring the water and ⅛ teaspoon salt to boiling; gradually stir in polenta. Reduce heat; cook and stir 5 to 8 minutes or until desired consistency. Stir in the remaining 1 tablespoon rosemary and 2 tablespoons of the Parmesan cheese.

4. Divide polenta among 6 serving plates; sprinkle with remaining 2 tablespoons Parmesan cheese. Serve roasted vegetables with polenta. **MAKES 6 SERVINGS**

Farro-White Bean Cups

START TO FINISH: 25 minutes

NUTRITION FACTS PER SERVING

Calories 277
Fat 11 g
Cholesterol 0 mg
Sodium 463 mg
Carbohydrates 36 g
Fiber 10 g
Protein 10 g

1   15-ounce can cannellini beans (white kidney beans), rinsed and drained
1   cup packaged precooked plain farro, such as Archer Farms Brand, or packaged cooked whole grain brown rice
½   cup carrot cut into matchstick-size strips
¼   cup coarsely chopped salted dry-roasted pistachio nuts
3   tablespoons oil-packed dried tomatoes, drained and chopped
3   tablespoons chopped red onion

1   avocado, halved, seeded, and peeled
2   tablespoons lime juice
1   teaspoon olive oil
1   clove garlic, minced
¼   teaspoon salt
¼   teaspoon dried Italian seasoning, crushed
8   large butterhead (Boston or Bibb) lettuce leaves or 4 small sweet red peppers, halved lengthwise and seeded

1. In a medium bowl combine cannellini beans, farro, carrot, pistachio nuts, tomatoes, and onion. Cube the avocado and toss with the lime juice. Add the avocado to the bean mixture; toss gently.

2. In a small bowl whisk together oil, garlic, salt, and Italian seasoning. Drizzle over bean mixture. Toss gently to combine.

3. Spoon about ½ cup of the bean mixture onto each lettuce leaf or spoon into sweet pepper halves.
MAKES 4 SERVINGS

Creamy Farro-Smothered Portobellos

START TO FINISH: 30 minutes

NUTRITION FACTS PER SERVING

Calories 215
Fat 6 g
Cholesterol 12 mg
Sodium 482 mg
Carbohydrates 28 g
Fiber 3 g
Protein 12 g

---

3 cups reduced-sodium vegetable broth
1 cup semi-pearled farro
6 5-inch fresh portobello mushrooms, stems and gills removed
   Nonstick cooking spray
2 cups coarsely chopped fresh Swiss chard leaves
¼ cup snipped dried tomatoes (not oil-pack)
2 teaspoons snipped fresh thyme or ½ teaspoon dried thyme, crushed
4 ounces soft goat cheese (chèvre), cut up
¼ cup finely shredded or shaved Parmesan cheese (1 ounce)
¼ cup sliced green onion tops
   Freshly ground black pepper

1. In a medium saucepan bring broth to boiling; slowly stir in farro. Return to boiling; reduce heat. Simmer, covered, for 15 minutes.

2. Meanwhile, lightly coat both sides of mushrooms with cooking spray. Preheat a grill pan over medium heat. Add mushrooms. Cook for 8 to 10 minutes or until tender, turning once.

3. Stir Swiss chard, dried tomatoes, and thyme into farro. Cook, covered, for 5 to 10 minutes more or until farro is tender. Remove from heat. Stir in goat cheese until melted.

4. To serve, place mushrooms, stemmed sides up, on a serving platter. Spoon farro mixture into mushrooms. Sprinkle with Parmesan cheese, green onion tops, and pepper. **MAKES 6 SERVINGS**

Gnocchi, Sweet Corn, and Arugula in Cream Sauce

START TO FINISH: **20 minutes**

NUTRITION FACTS PER SERVING

Calories 292   *Fat* 6 g   *Cholesterol* 18 mg   *Sodium* 797 mg   *Carbohydrates* 52 g   *Fiber* 1 g   *Protein* 9 g

1   pound shelf-stable potato gnocchi
2   fresh small ears sweet corn or 2 cups frozen whole kernel corn
¾   cup fat-free half-and-half or milk
3   ounces reduced-fat cream cheese (Neufchâtel), cut up
½   teaspoon garlic powder
½   teaspoon dried basil or oregano, crushed
¼   teaspoon salt
¼   teaspoon freshly ground black pepper
5   cups torn fresh arugula
    Crushed red pepper (optional)

1. In a large pot cook gnocchi according to package directions, adding corn the last 5 minutes of cooking time. Using tongs, transfer ears of corn (if using) to cutting board. Drain gnocchi and corn kernels (if using), reserving ¼ cup of the pasta water. Do not rinse.

2. Meanwhile, for cream sauce, in a medium saucepan combine half-and-half, cream cheese, garlic powder, basil, salt, and black pepper. Cook over medium heat for 5 minutes, stirring frequently. Stir in the reserved pasta water.

3. Return cooked pasta to pot. Pour cream sauce over pasta; heat through if necessary. Stir in arugula. Cut corn from cobs; add to pasta. Serve in bowls. If desired, sprinkle with crushed red pepper and additional dried basil or oregano. **MAKES 4 SERVINGS**

Tip: If you like, replace the corn with 1 cup chopped red sweet pepper and add 12 ounces cooked shrimp after tossing gnocchi with the cream sauce.

Vegetable Strudel

PREP: 40 minutes
BAKE: 25 minutes
STAND: 10 minutes
OVEN: 375°F

NUTRITION FACTS PER SERVING

Calories 182
Fat 5 g
Cholesterol 4 mg
Sodium 466 mg
Carbohydrates 29 g
Fiber 4 g
Protein 8 g

5   cups fresh spinach leaves
2   medium red sweet peppers, cut into 1-inch strips
1   medium yellow summer squash, cut into 1-inch strips
2   carrots, shredded
½   cup sliced fresh mushrooms
½   cup sliced green onions (4)
¼   cup oil-packed dried tomatoes, drained and chopped
3   tablespoons grated Parmesan cheese
1   tablespoon snipped fresh oregano or ½ teaspoon dried oregano, crushed
⅛   teaspoon salt
⅛   teaspoon ground black pepper
     Dash ground red pepper
     Butter-flavor nonstick spray
6   sheets frozen phyllo dough, thawed
2   tablespoons fine dry bread crumbs

1. Preheat oven to 375°F. For filling, place the spinach in a large colander; set aside. In a large saucepan cook sweet peppers, summer squash, carrots, mushrooms, and green onions in 4 cups boiling water for 2 to 3 minutes. Pour over spinach to drain; rinse immediately with cold water. Drain well, pressing out excess moisture. Transfer vegetables to a large bowl. Stir in the dried tomatoes, 2 tablespoons of the Parmesan cheese, the oregano, salt, black pepper, and ground red pepper. Set filling aside.

2. Spray a large baking sheet with nonstick spray. Place 1 sheet of phyllo on a dry kitchen towel. (Keep remaining sheets covered with plastic wrap to prevent drying out.) Spray with nonstick spray. Place another sheet on top; spray with nonstick spray. Sprinkle with half the bread crumbs. Place two more sheets of phyllo on top, spraying each with nonstick spray. Sprinkle with remaining crumbs. Add the remaining two sheets of phyllo, spraying each with nonstick spray.

3. For strudel, spoon filling along one long side of phyllo stack, about 1½ inches from edges. Fold in the short sides over the filling. Starting from the long side with filling, roll pastry into a spiral.

4. Place strudel, seam side down, on the prepared baking sheet. Spray top with nonstick spray. Using a sharp knife, score into 8 slices, cutting through the top layer only. Sprinkle with remaining Parmesan cheese.

5. Bake for 25 to 30 minutes or until the strudel is golden. Let stand for 10 minutes before serving. To serve, cut along scored lines into slices. **MAKES 4 SERVINGS**

CHAPTER 9 | Soups

Sunday Dinner Stew

START TO FINISH: 25 minutes

NUTRITION FACTS
PER SERVING

Calories 302
Fat 9 g
Cholesterol 52 mg
Sodium 686 mg
Carbohydrates 36 g
Fiber 6 g
Protein 22 g

1   pound small new potatoes
3   large carrots, halved
     lengthwise and/or cut up
1   17-ounce package refrigerated
     cooked beef tips with gravy
1¼ cups water
1   bunch green onions, chopped
     Fresh thyme (optional)

1. Scrub potatoes. Halve or quarter large potatoes so all pieces are about the same size. Place potatoes in a large microwave-safe bowl. Cover with vented plastic wrap. Microwave on 100 percent power (high) for 5 minutes. Add carrots; cover and microwave for 5 to 7 minutes or just until potatoes and carrots are tender.

2. In a 4-quart Dutch oven combine potatoes and carrots, beef tips in gravy, and the water. Cook over medium-high heat just until bubbly around edges. Add green onions. Cover and cook about 5 minutes more or until heated through. Ladle into bowls. If desired, sprinkle with thyme.
MAKES 4 SERVINGS

Sunday Dinner Sweet Potato and Kale Stew: Prepare as directed, except substitute 1 pound sweet potatoes, peeled and cut up, for the new potatoes. Add 1 cup chopped kale with the green onions.

Beef Stew with Garlic Mash

START TO FINISH: 25 minutes

NUTRITION FACTS
PER SERVING

Calories 368
Fat 14 g
Cholesterol 47 mg
Sodium 888 mg
Carbohydrates 42 g
Fiber 8 g
Protein 24 g

1   1-pound package frozen vegetable blend (carrots, peas, and onions)
½   cup water
1   17-ounce package refrigerated cooked beef tips in gravy
2   teaspoons Worcestershire sauce
6   cloves garlic
2   tablespoons water
1   pound Yukon gold or red potatoes, halved
2   tablespoons olive oil
¼   teaspoon salt
¼   teaspoon ground black pepper
2   tablespoons fresh oregano leaves

1. In a 4-quart Dutch oven combine frozen vegetables and the ½ cup water. Bring to boiling. Meanwhile, microwave beef tips according to package directions. Add beef and Worcestershire sauce to vegetables in Dutch oven. Reduce heat to low. Cook, covered, for 5 minutes or until vegetables are tender.

2. In a small microwave-safe bowl combine garlic and the 2 tablespoons water; cover with vented plastic wrap. Microwave on 100 percent power (high) for 1 minute; set aside. In a large microwave-safe bowl microwave potatoes on 100 percent power (high) for 8 to 10 minutes, stirring once.

3. Peel and mash garlic. Add garlic, olive oil, salt, and pepper to potatoes. Mash with a potato masher or beat with an electric mixer on low speed. Divide potatoes among four dishes; top with stew and sprinkle with oregano. **MAKES 4 SERVINGS**

Beefy Vegetable Soup

START TO FINISH: 30 minutes

NUTRITION FACTS PER SERVING

Calories 306   *Fat* 12 g   *Cholesterol* 74 mg   *Sodium* 747 mg   *Carbohydrates* 21 g   *Fiber* 4 g   *Protein* 27 g

1½ pounds lean ground beef
1   cup chopped onion (1 large)
1   cup sliced celery (2 stalks)
2   14.5-ounce cans lower-sodium
    beef broth
1   28-ounce can diced tomatoes,
    undrained
1   10-ounce package frozen
    mixed vegetables
2   tablespoons steak sauce
2   teaspoons Worcestershire
    sauce
¼   teaspoon salt
¼   teaspoon ground black pepper
¼   cup all-purpose flour

1. In a 4-quart Dutch oven cook ground beef, onion, and celery over medium-high heat until meat is browned, using a wooden spoon to break up meat as it cooks. Drain off fat.

2. Stir in 1 can of the broth, the tomatoes, frozen vegetables, steak sauce, Worcestershire sauce, salt, and pepper. Bring to boiling; reduce heat. Simmer, covered, for 15 to 20 minutes or until vegetables are tender.

3. In a medium bowl whisk together the remaining can of broth and flour; stir into soup. Cook and stir until thickened and bubbly. Cook and stir for 1 minute more. **MAKES 6 SERVINGS**

Adobo Black Bean Chili

PREP: 20 minutes
COOK: 20 minutes

NUTRITION FACTS
PER SERVING

Calories 317
Fat 7 g
Cholesterol 59 mg
Sodium 184 mg
Carbohydrates 35 g
Fiber 10 g
Protein 28 g

12   ounces 95% lean ground beef
½   cup chopped onion
     (1 medium)
¾   cup chopped green sweet
     pepper (1 medium)
2   cloves garlic, minced
1   15-ounce can no-salt added
     black beans, rinsed and
     drained, or 1¾ cups cooked
     black beans
1   14.5-ounce can no-salt-added
     diced tomatoes, undrained
1   8-ounce can no-salt-added
     tomato sauce
½   cup frozen whole kernel corn
1   tablespoon canned chipotle
     chile peppers in adobo sauce,
     finely chopped (see tip,
     page 114)

2   teaspoons chili powder
1   teaspoon dried oregano,
     crushed
1   teaspoon ground cumin
¼   teaspoon ground black pepper
2   tablespoons shredded
     reduced-fat cheddar cheese
¼   cup light sour cream

1. In a 4-quart Dutch oven cook ground beef, onion, sweet pepper, and garlic until meat is browned and onion is tender; drain off fat. Stir in beans, diced tomatoes, tomato sauce, corn, chile peppers, chili powder, oregano, cumin, and black pepper. Bring to boiling; reduce heat. Simmer, covered, for 20 minutes, stirring occasionally.

2. Top each serving with cheese and sour cream. MAKES 4 SERVINGS

Green Chile Pork Stew

START TO FINISH: 30 minutes

NUTRITION FACTS PER SERVING

Calories 297
Fat 11 g
Cholesterol 74 mg
Sodium 823 mg
Carbohydrates 21 g
Fiber 7 g
Protein 30 g

1   1-pound pork tenderloin
    Salt
    Ground black pepper
1   tablespoon olive oil
3   7-ounce packages frozen
    yellow carrots, spinach, and
    white bean medley in garlic-
    herb sauce,* thawed
1   4.5-ounce can diced green
    chiles, undrained
1   teaspoon ground cumin
1   cup water
    Fresh cilantro (optional)
    Lime wedges (optional)

1. Cut pork into ¾-inch pieces; sprinkle lightly with salt and pepper. In a 4-quart Dutch oven heat the olive oil over medium-high heat. Add pork; cook for 4 to 5 minutes or until browned. Stir in two of the packages of thawed vegetables, the chiles, and the cumin.

2. To puree vegetables, in a food processor or blender combine the remaining package of thawed vegetables and the water. Cover and process or blend until smooth.

3. Add pureed vegetables to stew in Dutch oven. Bring to boiling; reduce heat. Simmer, covered, about 15 minutes or until pork is cooked through, stirring occasionally.

4. Ladle stew into soup bowls. If desired, top with cilantro and serve with lime wedges.
MAKES 4 SERVINGS

Tip: To make a frozen vegetable blend, in a medium bowl stir together one 15-ounce can navy beans, rinsed and drained; 1 cup frozen sliced carrots, thawed; half a 10-ounce package frozen chopped spinach, thawed and well drained; and ¼ cup bottled Italian vinaigrette salad dressing. Stir 2 cups of the vegetable blend into the pork with the chiles and cumin. Puree the remaining blend with the 1 cup water. Continue as directed in Step 3.

Ham and Vegetable Soup

START TO FINISH: 30 minutes

NUTRITION FACTS PER SERVING

Calories 176   *Fat* 4 g   *Cholesterol* 19 mg   *Sodium* 586 mg   *Carbohydrates* 21 g   *Fiber* 6 g   *Protein* 14 g

2   teaspoons canola oil
1   cup cubed low-fat, reduced-
    sodium cooked ham
    (5 ounces)
2   cups water
1   14.5-ounce can reduced-
    sodium chicken broth
12 ounces fresh peas or one
    10-ounce package frozen
    baby peas
1   cup sliced carrots (2 medium)
1   cup sliced celery (2 stalks)
⅓   cup diagonally sliced green
    onions
1   tablespoon snipped fresh
    tarragon or ½ teaspoon dried
    tarragon, crushed
    Lemon wedges
½   of a 6-ounce carton plain
    fat-free yogurt

1. In a large saucepan heat oil over medium heat. Add ham; cook, without stirring, over medium heat for 3 minutes. Stir ham; cook for 2 to 3 minutes more or until browned.

2. Add the water, broth, peas, carrots, celery, green onions, and tarragon to ham. Bring to boiling; reduce heat. Simmer, covered, for 5 to 10 minutes or until peas and carrots are tender. Serve with lemon wedges and yogurt.
MAKES 4 SERVINGS

Creamy Asparagus and Bacon Soup

START TO FINISH: **30 minutes**

NUTRITION FACTS PER SERVING

Calories 356
Fat 15 g
Cholesterol 41 mg
Sodium 673 mg
Carbohydrates 43 g
Fiber 4 g
Protein 15 g

1¼ pounds fresh asparagus
    spears, trimmed
1   12-ounce can evaporated milk
1¼ cups water
1¼ pounds potatoes, peeled and
    cut into ½-inch pieces
½   teaspoon salt
½   teaspoon ground black pepper
6   slices bacon
1   tablespoon honey
    Toppings, such as finely
    shredded lemon peel, snipped
    fresh Italian (flat-leaf)
    parsley, coarse salt, and/or
    freshly ground black pepper

1. Set aside about one-third of the asparagus. In a large saucepan combine the remaining asparagus, evaporated milk, the water, potatoes, the ½ teaspoon salt, and the ½ teaspoon pepper. Bring to boiling; reduce heat. Simmer, covered, about 10 minutes or until potatoes are tender. Cool slightly.

2. Transfer potato mixture, half at a time, to a food processor or blender. Cover and process or blend until smooth.

3. Meanwhile, in a large skillet cook bacon over medium heat until crisp. Remove bacon and drain on paper towels, reserving 1 tablespoon drippings in skillet.

Crumble bacon; set aside. Add the reserved asparagus to drippings in skillet. Cook for 5 to 6 minutes or until asparagus is crisp-tender, stirring occasionally.

4. Before serving, place crumbled bacon in a microwave-safe pie plate. Drizzle with honey; cover with vented plastic wrap. Microwave on 100 percent power (high) for 30 seconds.

5. Ladle soup into bowls. Top each serving with asparagus, honey-drizzled bacon, and your choice of toppings. **MAKES 4 SERVINGS**

Fresh Corn and Chicken Chowder

START TO FINISH: **30 minutes**

NUTRITION FACTS PER SERVING

Calories 269
Fat 3 g
Cholesterol 54 mg
Sodium 721 mg
Carbohydrates 33 g
Fiber 3 g
Protein 29 g

12 ounces skinless, boneless chicken breast halves or chicken thighs
4 fresh ears corn
1 32-ounce box reduced-sodium chicken broth
½ cup chopped green sweet pepper (1 small)
1¼ cups instant mashed potato flakes
1 cup milk
Salt
Ground black pepper
Crushed red pepper (optional)

1. In a 4-quart Dutch oven combine chicken, corn, and broth. Bring to boiling; reduce heat. Simmer, covered, about 12 minutes or until chicken is no longer pink. Transfer chicken and corn to a cutting board.

2. Add ¼ cup of the sweet pepper to broth in Dutch oven. Stir in potato flakes and milk. Using two forks, shred chicken. Return chicken to Dutch oven.

3. Using a kitchen towel to hold hot corn, cut kernels or planks of corn from cobs. Add corn to chowder in Dutch oven; heat through. Season with salt and black pepper. Top each serving with some of the remaining chopped sweet pepper. If desired, sprinkle with crushed red pepper. **MAKES 4 SERVINGS**

Make-Ahead Directions:
Prepare chowder as directed; let cool. Transfer chowder to an airtight container. Cover and refrigerate for up to 3 days. Reheat chowder in a Dutch oven over medium heat until heated through.

Spring Chicken Stew

START TO FINISH: 30 minutes

NUTRITION FACTS PER SERVING

Calories 273   *Fat* 12 g   *Cholesterol* 117 mg   *Sodium* 909 mg   *Carbohydrates* 13 g   *Fiber* 3 g   *Protein* 31 g

1   lemon
1¼ pounds skinless, boneless
     chicken thighs
     Salt
     Ground black pepper
1   tablespoon olive oil
1½ cups water
1   12-ounce jar chicken gravy
8   ounces whole baby carrots,
     halved lengthwise
1   tablespoon Dijon mustard
2   heads baby bok choy,
     quartered
     Snipped fresh lemon thyme
     (optional)

1. Finely shred peel from lemon; set peel aside. Juice lemon and set juice aside. Lightly sprinkle chicken with salt and pepper.

2. In a 4-quart Dutch oven heat olive oil over medium-high heat; add chicken. Cook for 2 to 3 minutes or until chicken is browned, turning occasionally.

3. Add the water, gravy, carrots, and mustard to chicken in Dutch oven. Bring to boiling. Place bok choy on top. Reduce heat. Simmer, covered, about 10 minutes or until chicken is no longer pink and vegetables are tender. Add lemon juice to taste.

4. Ladle stew into bowls. Top with lemon peel and, if desired, lemon thyme. **MAKES 4 SERVINGS**

Cream of Fennel and Potato Soup

START TO FINISH: 30 minutes

NUTRITION FACTS
PER SERVING

Calories 254
Fat 9 g
Cholesterol 39 mg
Sodium 831 mg
Carbohydrates 29 g
Fiber 7 g
Protein 17 g

1 tablespoon olive oil
3 cups chopped fennel
  (1½ pounds)
¾ cup chopped yellow onion
1 clove garlic, minced
2½ cups reduced-sodium chicken
  broth
8 ounces yellow-flesh potatoes,
  peeled and sliced
¾ cup fat-free milk
¼ teaspoon dried thyme,
  crushed
8 ounces uncooked bulk turkey
  Italian sausage
1½ teaspoons lemon juice
  Slivered green onions
  (optional)

1. In a large saucepan heat oil over medium heat. Add fennel, yellow onion, and garlic; cook for 5 to 6 minutes or until fennel and onion are tender, stirring occasionally. Add broth, potatoes, milk, and thyme. Bring to boiling; reduce heat. Simmer, covered, for 10 to 15 minutes or until potatoes are tender. Cool slightly.

2. Meanwhile, in a medium nonstick skillet cook sausage over medium heat until browned, using a wooden spoon to break up sausage as it cooks. Drain off fat.

3. Transfer potato soup, half at a time, to a food processor or blender. Cover and process or blend until smooth. Return soup to saucepan. Stir in sausage and lemon juice; heat through.

4. Ladle soup into serving bowls. If desired, sprinkle with green onions. **MAKES 4 SERVINGS**

Shrimp Cocktail Soup

START TO FINISH: 30 minutes

NUTRITION FACTS PER SERVING

Calories 109
Fat 1 g
Cholesterol 111 mg
Sodium 734 mg
Carbohydrates 11 g
Fiber 2 g
Protein 16 g

3   cups peeled, seeded, and chopped ripe tomatoes (6 medium)
1¾ cups peeled, seeded, and chopped cucumber (1 medium)
½   cup finely chopped green sweet pepper (1 small)
⅓   cup finely chopped red onion (1 small)
2   cloves garlic, minced
2   cups tomato juice
1   14.5-ounce can reduced-sodium chicken broth
¼   cup red wine vinegar
2   tablespoons snipped fresh basil or 2 teaspoons dried basil, crushed
½   teaspoon salt
¼   to ½ teaspoon bottled hot pepper sauce
¼   teaspoon ground black pepper
12 ounces chopped, peeled, and deveined cooked shrimp
    Lime slices (optional)

1. In an extra-large bowl combine tomatoes, cucumber, sweet pepper, red onion, and garlic. Stir in tomato juice, broth, vinegar, basil, salt, hot pepper sauce, and black pepper. Stir in shrimp.

2. Ladle soup into mugs or bowls. If desired, serve with slices of lime.
MAKES 6 SERVINGS

Make-Ahead Directions: Prepare as directed, except do not add shrimp. Cover soup and chill for up to 24 hours. Before serving, stir in shrimp.

Easy Cioppino

START TO FINISH: 30 minutes

NUTRITION FACTS PER SERVING

Calories 178   *Fat* 6 g   *Cholesterol* 49 mg   *Sodium* 169 mg   *Carbohydrates* 9 g   *Fiber* 3 g   *Protein* 22 g

2   pounds fresh or frozen skinless salmon, cod, and/or sea scallops
3   tablespoons olive oil
2   fennel bulbs, trimmed and thinly sliced
4   cloves garlic, minced
3   cups coarsely chopped tomatoes (3 large)
1   14- to 15-ounce can fish stock or chicken broth
2   teaspoons snipped fresh oregano or 1 teaspoon dried oregano, crushed
½   teaspoon anise seeds, crushed (optional)
     Salt
     Freshly ground black pepper
     Fennel leaves or shredded fresh basil (optional)

1. Thaw fish and/or scallops, if frozen. Rinse fish and/or scallops; pat dry with paper towels. If using fish, cut into 2-inch pieces. Set fish and scallops aside.

2. In a 4- to 6-quart Dutch oven heat olive oil over medium heat. Add sliced fennel; cook about 10 minutes or until tender, stirring occasionally. Add garlic; cook and stir for 1 minute more.

3. Add tomatoes, fish stock, dried oregano (if using), and, if desired, anise seeds to fennel mixture in Dutch oven. Bring to boiling. Stir in fish and/or scallops. Return to boiling; reduce heat. Simmer, uncovered, for 6 to 8 minutes or until fish flakes easily when tested with a fork and scallops are opaque.

4. Season with salt and pepper. Stir in fresh oregano (if using). If desired, top individual servings with fennel leaves.
MAKES 8 SERVINGS

Curried Vegetable Soup

START TO FINISH: 20 minutes

NUTRITION FACTS PER SERVING

Calories 138
Fat 6 g
Cholesterol 0 mg
Sodium 620 mg
Carbohydrates 19 g
Fiber 4 g
Protein 3 g

3   cups cauliflower florets
1   14.5-ounce can vegetable
      broth
1   14-ounce can unsweetened
      coconut milk
¼   cup snipped fresh cilantro
1   tablespoon curry powder
¼   teaspoon salt
2   cups frozen baby peas and
      vegetables blend
      Crushed red pepper
      (optional)
      Snipped fresh cilantro
      (optional)
1   recipe Curry Pita Crisps
      (optional)

1. In a 4-quart Dutch oven combine cauliflower, broth, coconut milk, the ¼ cup cilantro, the curry powder, and salt. Bring to boiling; reduce heat. Simmer, covered, about 10 minutes or until cauliflower is tender. Stir in frozen vegetables; heat through.

2. Ladle soup into bowls. If desired, sprinkle with crushed red pepper and additional cilantro. Serve with Curry Pita Crisps. **MAKES 4 SERVINGS**

Curry Pita Crisps: Preheat broiler. Cut two pita bread rounds into wedges. Brush both sides of wedges with 1 tablespoon olive oil; place on a large baking sheet. Sprinkle with ¼ teaspoon curry powder. Broil 3 to 4 inches from heat about 4 minutes or until golden, turning once.

Roasted Root Vegetable Soup

PREP: 30 minutes
ROAST: 35 minutes
OVEN: 425°F

NUTRITION FACTS PER SERVING

Calories 191
Fat 4 g
Cholesterol 4 mg
Sodium 359 mg
Carbohydrates 3 g
Fiber 3 g
Protein 9 g

2   carrots, peeled and cut into 1-inch chunks
1   sweet potato, peeled and cut into 1-inch cubes
1   parsnip, peeled and cut into 1-inch chunks
½   of a red onion, cut into thin wedges
3   cloves garlic, thinly sliced
1   tablespoon olive oil
1   teaspoon dried thyme, crushed
⅛   teaspoon ground black pepper
3   cups fat-free milk
1   cup reduced-sodium chicken broth
¼   cup all-purpose flour

1. Preheat oven to 425°F. In a 13×9×2-inch baking pan combine carrots, sweet potato, parsnip, red onion, and garlic. Drizzle with oil; sprinkle with half the thyme and all the pepper. Toss to coat. Cover with foil.

2. Roast for 20 minutes. Remove foil; stir vegetables. Roast, uncovered, for 15 to 20 minutes more or until vegetables are tender.

3. Meanwhile, in a large saucepan whisk together milk, chicken broth, flour, and the remaining thyme until smooth. Cook and stir over medium heat until thickened and bubbly. Add roasted vegetables. Cook and stir about 1 minute more or until heated through. **MAKES 4 SERVINGS**

Garden Vegetable Gazpacho

START TO FINISH: 20 minutes

NUTRITION FACTS PER SERVING

Calories 41   *Fat* 1 g   *Cholesterol* 162 mg   *Sodium* 162 mg   *Carbohydrates* 9 g   *Fiber* 2 g   *Protein* 2 g

2¼ cups chopped, peeled
   tomatoes (3 medium)
½ cup chopped yellow or green
   sweet pepper
¼ thinly sliced green onions (2)
1 tablespoon snipped fresh basil
   or ½ teaspoon dried basil,
   crushed
1 clove garlic, minced
1 5.5-ounce can reduced-sodium
   tomato juice
½ cup reduced-sodium chicken
   broth or vegetable broth
1 tablespoon lemon juice
   Dash freshly ground black
   pepper
   Several dashes bottled hot
   pepper sauce
   Fresh basil leaves (optional)
⅛ teaspoon salt

1. In a large bowl combine
tomatoes, sweet pepper, green
onions, basil, and garlic. Stir in
tomato juice, chicken broth,
lemon juice, pepper, and hot
pepper sauce.

2. To serve, ladle soup into chilled
soup bowls or mugs. If desired,
garnish with basil leaves.
MAKES 4 SERVINGS

Make-Ahead Directions:
Prepare as directed. Cover and
chill for up to 24 hours.

Tomato-Basil Soup with Toasted Cheese Croutons

PREP: 25 minutes
COOK: 10 minutes

NUTRITION FACTS PER SERVING

Calories 94
Fat 3 g
Cholesterol 3 mg
Sodium 267 mg
Carbohydrates 1 g
Fiber 3 g
Protein 3 g

- 1   medium onion, chopped
- 2   cloves garlic, minced
- 2   teaspoons olive oil
- 2   14.5-ounce cans no-salt-added diced tomatoes
- 1½ cups ⅓-less-sodium vegetable broth or reduced-sodium chicken broth
- ¾   cup jarred roasted red sweet peppers, drained and chopped
- 2   tablespoons snipped fresh basil or 2 teaspoons dried basil, crushed
- 2   teaspoons balsamic vinegar
- 1   recipe Toasted Cheese Croutons

1. In a medium nonstick saucepan cook onion and garlic in hot oil about 5 minutes or until tender, stirring occasionally. Add undrained tomatoes, vegetable broth, roasted peppers, and dried basil (if using). Bring to boiling; reduce heat. Cover and simmer for 10 minutes to blend flavors. Cool slightly.

2. Transfer half the soup mixture to a blender or food processor. Cover and blend or process until smooth; return to soup in saucepan. Heat through. Stir in fresh basil (if using). Stir in vinegar just before serving. Top each serving with a few Toasted Cheese Croutons.
MAKES 6 SERVINGS

Toasted Cheese Croutons: Place four ¾-inch slices whole grain baguette-style bread or regular baguette on a small baking sheet. Broil 4 to 5 inches from the heat for 1 to 2 minutes or until lightly toasted. Turn bread slices over; sprinkle with ¼ cup shredded reduced-fat Italian cheese blend. Broil about 1 minute more or until cheese is melted. Cool bread slices slightly. Cut into irregular bite-size pieces.

CHAPTER 10

Sides

Harvest Slaw

START TO FINISH: 30 minutes

NUTRITION FACTS
PER SERVING

Calories 108
Fat 7 g
Cholesterol 0 mg
Sodium 56 mg
Carbohydrates 13 g
Fiber 2 g
Protein 1 g

3   tablespoons olive oil
2   garlic cloves, coarsely
    chopped
2   teaspoons caraway seeds,
    lightly crushed
¼   cup cider vinegar
1   tablespoon honey
    Salt and ground black pepper
4   cups finely shredded red
    and/or green cabbage
2   red apples, cored and thinly
    sliced
½   cup dried cranberries
½   cup pecan halves, toasted (see
    tip, page 178)
2   tablespoons cilantro or
    parsley leaves

1. For dressing, in a large skillet heat olive oil over medium heat. Add garlic and caraway seeds; cook and stir for 1 minute. Whisk in vinegar and honey. Heat and stir just until mixture comes to simmering. Remove from heat. Season with salt and pepper.

2. In a large bowl toss together cabbage, apples, cranberries, and pecans. Pour dressing over slaw; toss to combine. Sprinkle with cilantro. **MAKES 12 SERVINGS**

Spicy Ginger-Carrot Slaw

START TO FINISH: 25 minutes

NUTRITION FACTS
PER SERVING

Calories 118
Fat 7 g
Cholesterol 0 mg
Sodium 31 mg
Carbohydrates 11 g
Fiber 3 g
Protein 2 g

1   small head napa cabbage, core
    removed, shredded
2   medium red sweet peppers,
    cut into bite-size strips
4   to 6 medium carrots,
    shredded
1   pink grapefruit, sectioned
4   green onions, slivered
1   recipe Lime Dressing

1. In a large glass bowl layer cabbage, sweet peppers, carrots, and grapefruit. If desired, cover and chill up to 24 hours.

2. Just before serving, add green onions. Add about half the dressing, toss. Pass the remaining dressing. **MAKES 8 SERVINGS**

Lime Dressing: In a small screw-top jar combine ¼ cup olive oil; 2 to 4 tablespoons tequila; ½-inch piece fresh ginger, peeled and finely chopped; 1 teaspoon finely shredded lime peel; 2 tablespoons lime juice and peel; and ½ teaspoon crushed red pepper. Cover and shake to combine. If desired, let stand at room temperature for 1 hour; shake again before drizzling over salad.

Peach and Blackberry Slaw

START TO FINISH: 30 minutes

NUTRITION FACTS PER SERVING

Calories 151   *Fat* 9 g   *Cholesterol* 0 mg   *Sodium* 116 mg   *Carbohydrates* 16 g   *Fiber* 5 g   *Protein* 2 g

¼ cup white wine vinegar
¼ cup olive oil
1 tablespoon snipped fresh chives, basil, and/or tarragon
1 teaspoon sugar
   Salt
   Ground black pepper
1 small head cabbage
3 fresh peaches
½ pint blackberries
2 ounces blue cheese, coarsely crumbled (optional)
   Snipped fresh chives, parsley, basil, and/or tarragon (optional)

1. For dressing, in a small bowl whisk together vinegar, oil, the 1 tablespoon chives, and the sugar. Season with salt and pepper; set aside.

2. Shred cabbage and place in a large bowl. Halve, pit, and thinly slice peaches; add to bowl with cabbage. Gently toss to combine. Drizzle with half the dressing; toss to coat. Top with blackberries and, if desired, crumbled cheese. If desired, sprinkle with additional chives. Pass the remaining dressing. **MAKES 6 SERVINGS**

Fresh Asparagus Ribbon Salad

START TO FINISH: 30 minutes

NUTRITION FACTS PER SERVING

Calories 73
Fat 6 g
Cholesterol 3 mg
Sodium 73 mg
Carbohydrates 4 g
Fiber 2 g
Protein 2 g

1   pound thick green, purple, or white asparagus (about 14 spears)
2   cloves garlic, peeled
½   teaspoon kosher salt
½   cup sour cream
⅓   cup olive oil
3   to 4 tablespoons lemon juice
½   cup snipped fresh Italian (flat-leaf) parsley
¼   cup snipped fresh chives
1   tablespoon milk (optional)
    Ground black pepper
1   head Bibb lettuce, torn (6 cups)
½   English (seedless) cucumber, thinly sliced
3   radishes, very thinly sliced

1. Remove scales from asparagus spears.* Using a vegetable peeler, peel thin "ribbons" from the spears.** Place ribbons in a medium bowl of ice water; set aside.

2. Meanwhile, to make garlic paste, on a cutting board finely chop the garlic. Sprinkle with salt. Holding a large flat chef's knife at a slight angle, blade almost flat with cutting board, mash and rub the salt into the garlic.

3. For dressing, in a large bowl whisk together the garlic paste, sour cream, olive oil, and lemon juice. Stir in parsley and chives. If desired, thin with milk. Season with pepper.

4. Drain asparagus ribbons and pat dry (or spin in a salad spinner). On a platter arrange lettuce, asparagus ribbons and tips, cucumber slices, and radish slices.

Drizzle with dressing. Cover and chill any remaining dressing for up to 3 days. Stir dressing well before serving. **MAKES 6 SERVINGS**

*Tip: The dark triangular leaves, or scales, on asparagus spears can be especially tough on thick spears. To remove them, use a paring knife to peel them off. Discard the scales.

**Tip: Thin asparagus ribbons are easy to cut using a sharp vegetable peeler on thick asparagus spears. Trim the asparagus, then lay it flat on a work surface. Beginning from the stem or bottom end, peel toward the tips. Either take care to avoid snapping off the tender tips with the peeler or break off the tips to toss in the salad with the ribbons.

Caramelized Brussels Sprouts with Lemon

START TO FINISH: 20 minutes

NUTRITION FACTS PER SERVING

Calories 106
Fat 9 g
Cholesterol 0 mg
Sodium 209 mg
Carbohydrates 6 g
Fiber 2 g
Protein 2 g

¼ cup extra virgin olive oil
4 cups Brussels sprouts, rinsed, trimmed, and halved lengthwise (4 cups)*
  Salt and freshly ground black pepper
2 tablespoons water
1 tablespoon lemon juice

1. In an extra-large nonstick skillet heat 3 tablespoons of the oil over medium heat. Arrange sprouts in a single layer, cut sides down. Drizzle with the remaining olive oil; sprinkle with salt and pepper. Cook, covered, for 3 minutes. Remove lid and sprinkle sprouts with water. Cook, covered, for 2 minutes more. Sprouts should just be beginning to caramelize and, when pierced with a fork, slightly tender.

2. Remove lid and increase heat slightly. When cut sides are well-caramelized, toss Brussels sprouts in pan; drizzle with lemon juice.
MAKES 6 SERVINGS

*Tip: Fresh Brussels sprouts don't store particularly well. Use them within three days of purchasing for the best possible flavor and texture. Store, unwashed and untrimmed, in an airtight container in the refrigerator. Wash and trim right before use.

Broiled Bok Choy with Miso Sauce

PREP: 25 minutes
BROIL: 13 minutes

NUTRITION FACTS PER SERVING

Calories 108   *Fat* 5 g   *Cholesterol* 0 mg   *Sodium* 327 mg   *Carbohydrates* 15 g   *Fiber* 2 g   *Protein* 3 g

Nonstick cooking spray
4   teaspoons olive oil
6   baby bok choy (about
     1 pound), halved lengthwise
4   ounces fresh shiitake
     mushrooms, stemmed and
     halved lengthwise
2   tablespoons orange juice
2   tablespoons sweet rice wine
     (mirin)
1   tablespoon red miso paste
1   tablespoon honey
2   teaspoons grated fresh ginger
2   teaspoons finely shredded
     orange peel
1   to 2 teaspoons Asian chili
     sauce (Sriracha sauce)
     Orange slices, quartered
     (optional)

1. Preheat broiler. Coat a 15×10×1-inch baking pan with cooking spray; drizzle pan with 2 teaspoons of the oil. Add bok choy and mushrooms to pan; stir and toss to coat vegetables with oil.

2. For sauce, in a small bowl whisk together the remaining 2 teaspoons oil, orange juice, rice wine, miso paste, honey, ginger, orange peel, and chili sauce. Set aside.

3. Broil vegetables about 6 inches from the heat for 6 minutes. Turn bok choy over. Broil for 7 to 8 minutes more or until bok choy leaves are slightly charred and stems are crisp-tender.

4. Transfer bok choy and mushrooms to a serving platter. Drizzle sauce over vegetables. If desired, garnish with orange slices.
MAKES 4 SERVINGS

Braised Cabbage with Spicy Croutons

PREP: 10 minutes
COOK: 18 minutes

NUTRITION FACTS PER SERVING

Calories 141
Fat 7 g
Cholesterol 5 mg
Sodium 254 mg
Carbohydrates 19 g
Fiber 4 g
Protein 4 g

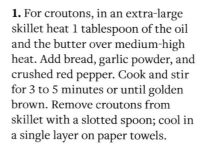

2 tablespoons olive oil
1 tablespoon butter
⅓ 12-ounce baguette, torn into coarse crumbs (2 cups)
¼ teaspoon garlic powder
¼ teaspoon crushed red pepper
1 small head green cabbage, cut into 6 wedges
  Salt and ground black pepper
½ cup water
  Snipped fresh parsley
  Lemon wedges

1. For croutons, in an extra-large skillet heat 1 tablespoon of the oil and the butter over medium-high heat. Add bread, garlic powder, and crushed red pepper. Cook and stir for 3 to 5 minutes or until golden brown. Remove croutons from skillet with a slotted spoon; cool in a single layer on paper towels.

2. Add cabbage to the skillet, overlapping wedges if necessary. Sprinkle with salt and black pepper. Add water; bring to boiling. Reduce heat; simmer, covered, about 15 minutes or until tender.

3. Place cabbage on a platter; drizzle the remaining 1 tablespoon olive oil over cabbage. Sprinkle with croutons and parsley; serve with lemon wedges.
MAKES 6 SERVINGS

Pumpkin Mashed Potatoes

PREP: 15 minutes
COOK: 20 minutes

NUTRITION FACTS PER SERVING

Calories 159
Fat 5 g
Cholesterol 13 mg
Sodium 206 mg
Carbohydrates 26 g
Fiber 4 g
Protein 4 g

1   pound medium baking potatoes, peeled and quartered
2   cloves garlic, peeled
1   cup canned pumpkin
2   tablespoons reduced-fat cream cheese (Neufchâtel)
1   tablespoon butter or tub-style vegetable oil spread
⅛   teaspoon ground sage
¼   teaspoon salt
¼   teaspoon ground pepper
¼   cup fat-free milk
1   recipe Miniature Pumpkin Bowls* (optional)
    Fresh sage leaves (optional)

1. In a large covered saucepan cook potatoes and garlic in enough boiling water to cover for 20 to 25 minutes or until potatoes are tender; drain. Mash with a potato masher or beat with an electric mixer on low speed until nearly smooth. Beat in canned pumpkin, cream cheese, butter, ground sage, salt, and pepper. Gradually add milk, beating until light and fluffy. Return to saucepan; heat through.

2. If desired, spoon mashed potatoes into Miniature Pumpkin Bowls and garnish with sage leaves. **MAKES 4 SERVINGS**

*Tip: To make Miniature Pumpkin Bowls, preheat oven to 325°F. Cut off ½ inch from the tops of 4 miniature pumpkins (6 to 8 ounces each); discard tops. Using a spoon, scoop out and discard seeds and membranes. Place pumpkins, cut sides down, on a baking sheet. Bake for 20 to 25 minutes or just until pumpkins are easily pierced with a fork yet still hold shape.

Sesame Kale and Edamame

START TO FINISH: 25 minutes

NUTRITION FACTS PER SERVING

Calories 111   *Fat* 4 g   *Cholesterol* 0 mg   *Sodium* 359 mg   *Carbohydrates* 15 g   *Fiber* 3 g   *Protein* 6 g

½ cup frozen shelled sweet soybeans (edamame)
1 bunch kale (about 12 ounces)
1 large red sweet pepper, seeded and cut into bite-size strips
2 tablespoons reduced-sodium soy sauce
1 tablespoon sweet rice wine (mirin)
2 teaspoons grated fresh ginger
2 teaspoons toasted sesame oil
1 teaspoon sesame seeds, toasted*

1. In a small saucepan cook edamame in boiling water for 3 to 4 minutes or until tender; drain and set aside. Remove and discard thick stems from kale. Chop or tear leaves into bite-size pieces (about 8 cups).

2. In a 4-quart Dutch oven cook kale and sweet pepper in boiling water for 30 seconds; drain. Transfer to a bowl of ice water for 1 minute; drain. Use a salad spinner to dry the kale and sweet pepper or pat dry with paper towels.

3. Place kale and pepper in a shallow serving bowl. For dressing, in a small bowl combine soy sauce, rice wine, ginger, and sesame oil. Drizzle dressing over salad. Sprinkle with sesame seeds. Serve immediately or cover and chill up to 2 hours. **MAKES 4 SERVINGS**

*Tip: To toast sesame seeds, scatter them in a dry small skillet and heat over medium heat just until golden. Stir frequently to prevent seeds from burning.

Sautéed Green Beans with Shallot Crisps

START TO FINISH: 30 minutes

NUTRITION FACTS PER SERVING

Calories 100
Fat 7 g
Cholesterol 4 mg
Sodium 18 mg
Carbohydrates 10 g
Fiber 4 g
Protein 2 g

⅓ cup canola oil
5 to 6 shallots, thinly sliced (½ cup)
2 pounds green beans, trimmed
1 tablespoon butter
1 tablespoon olive oil
    Salt and freshly ground black pepper

1. For shallot crisps, in a small skillet heat oil over medium-high heat.* Using a slotted spoon, add half the shallots. Fry for 3 to 4 minutes or until crisp and dark golden brown. Remove from oil; drain on paper towels. Repeat with remaining shallots. Set aside.

2. Meanwhile, in a large pot cook beans, covered, in enough boiling water to cover for 6 to 8 minutes or until crisp-tender. Drain and submerse in ice water to cool quickly; drain well.

3. Heat an extra-large skillet over medium-high heat. Add butter and oil, swirling to coat skillet. Add beans. Cook about 5 minutes or until beans are heated through, stirring frequently. Season beans with salt and pepper. Transfer to a serving bowl and top with shallot crisps. **MAKES 8 SERVINGS**

***Tip:** Test oil by adding 1 shallot slice to oil. When oil sizzles without spattering and shallot is golden, the oil is ready.

Make-Ahead Directions: Shallot crisps may be prepared up to 2 hours ahead.

Honey-Wasabi Mashed Peas

PREP: 10 minutes
COOK: 10 minutes

NUTRITION FACTS PER SERVING

Calories 76
Fat 0 g
Cholesterol 0 mg
Sodium 178 mg
Carbohydrates 15 g
Fiber 3 g
Protein 4 g

1	14- to 16-ounce package frozen peas
2	tablespoons honey
2	tablespoons lemon juice or rice vinegar
1	teaspoon prepared wasabi paste
1	small clove garlic, minced
¼	teaspoon salt
¼	teaspoon ground black pepper
	Lemon slices (optional)
	Watercress (optional

1. In a medium saucepan combine peas with enough water to cover. Bring to boiling; reduce heat. Simmer, uncovered, for 7 minutes or until very tender; drain.

2. Stir honey, lemon juice, wasabi paste, garlic, salt, and pepper into peas in saucepan. Cook for 3 minutes. Mash peas slightly with a potato masher or fork just until coarsely mashed. Top with lemon slices and watercress.

MAKES 6 SERVINGS

Brussels Sprouts and Noodle Stir-Fry with Cilantro and Almonds

START TO FINISH: 30 minutes

NUTRITION FACTS PER SERVING

Calories 115   *Fat* 5 g   *Cholesterol* 0 mg   *Sodium* 196 mg   *Carbohydrates* 15 g   *Fiber* 3 g   *Protein* 4 g

3   ounces dried whole wheat thin spaghetti
2   tablespoons olive oil
1   cup thinly sliced red onion
3   cloves garlic, minced
12 ounces Brussels sprouts, trimmed and thinly sliced or shredded
1   tablespoon grated fresh ginger
¼   to ½ teaspoon crushed red pepper
½   cup reduced-sodium chicken broth
2   tablespoons reduced-sodium soy sauce
½   cup shredded carrot (1 medium)
⅓   cup snipped fresh cilantro
3   tablespoons slivered almonds, toasted (see tip, page 178)

1. Break spaghetti into 1-inch pieces. Cook spaghetti according to package directions; drain. Return spaghetti to hot pan; cover and keep warm.

2. Pour oil into a large skillet; heat skillet over medium-high heat. Add onion and garlic; cook and stir for 1 minute. Add Brussels sprouts, ginger, and crushed red pepper; cook and stir for 1 minute. Add broth and soy sauce. Cook about 2 minutes more or until liquid is almost evaporated, stirring occasionally. Remove from heat.

3. Stir in cooked spaghetti, carrot, and cilantro. Before serving, sprinkle with almonds.
MAKES 8 SERVINGS

Herbed Garden Couscous

START TO FINISH: 30 minutes

NUTRITION FACTS
PER SERVING

Calories 196
Fat 11 g
Cholesterol 6 mg
Sodium 172 mg
Carbohydrates 21 g
Fiber 3 g
Protein 5 g

1 cup whole wheat or plain couscous
2 cups cherry tomatoes, halved
1 medium cucumber, coarsely chopped
1 medium green sweet pepper, coarsely chopped
½ cup snipped fresh chives
¼ cup snipped fresh Italian (flat-leaf) parsley
¼ cup snipped fresh mint
¼ cup snipped fresh oregano
⅓ cup balsamic vinegar
⅓ cup olive oil
2 teaspoons sugar
½ teaspoon salt
¼ teaspoon ground black pepper
½ cup crumbled feta cheese
½ cup coarsely chopped walnuts, toasted (see tip, page 178)

1. Cook the couscous according to package directions. Fluff with a fork.

2. Meanwhile, in a large bowl combine tomatoes, cucumber, sweet pepper, chives, parsley, mint, and oregano. Fold in couscous.

3. For dressing, in a small bowl whisk together the balsamic vinegar, olive oil, sugar, salt, and freshly ground black pepper. Pour over garden couscous and toss to combine. Spoon into serving bowl. To serve, top with feta cheese and toasted walnuts. **MAKES 12 SERVINGS**

Collard Greens with Lemon, Farro, and Feta

START TO FINISH: 30 minutes

NUTRITION FACTS
PER SERVING

Calories 115
Fat 4 g
Cholesterol 3 mg
Sodium 368 mg
Carbohydrates 14 g
Fiber 3 g
Protein 6 g

1   bunch collard greens, mustard greens, or Swiss chard (about 12 ounces)
½   cup semi-pearled farro
1   tablespoon olive oil
4   cloves garlic, minced
½   teaspoon salt
1   tablespoon finely shredded lemon peel
1   tablespoon lemon juice
½   cup crumbled reduced-fat feta cheese (2 ounces)
¼   cup snipped fresh parsley
    Lemon wedges (optional)

1. Remove and discard thick stems from collard greens. Chop leaves into bite-size pieces (about 8 cups). In a Dutch oven cook collard greens in boiling water about 7 minutes or until tender. Using a slotted spoon, transfer greens to a bowl of ice water for 1 minute; drain and set aside.

2. Stir farro into the boiling water. Cook about 10 minutes or until tender. Drain in a colander.

3. In the same Dutch oven heat oil over medium-high heat. Add garlic; cook and stir about 2 minutes or until golden. Stir in collard greens, farro, and salt; heat through. Stir in lemon peel and lemon juice.

4. Divide greens mixture among serving bowls. Sprinkle with cheese and parsley. If desired, serve with lemon wedges.
MAKES 6 SERVINGS

New Potato-Cabbage Salad

PREP: 25 minutes   COOK: 10 minutes   CHILL: 2 hours

NUTRITION FACTS PER SERVING

Calories 82   *Fat* 3 g   *Cholesterol* 5 mg   *Sodium* 220 mg   *Carbohydrates* 11 g   *Fiber* 2 g   *Protein* 2 g

12 ounces round red or small
    Yukon gold potatoes, cut into
    ½-inch-thick wedges
3   tablespoons light mayonnaise
2   tablespoons German mustard
3   tablespoons cider vinegar
3   cups shredded green cabbage*
1   cup shredded carrots*
1   stalk celery, thinly sliced
½   cup thinly sliced green onions
2   slices turkey bacon, cooked
    according to package
    directions, then chopped

1. In a large covered saucepan cook potato wedges in enough boiling water to cover for 10 to 12 minutes or until tender. Drain well; set aside to cool.

2. Meanwhile, in a large bowl whisk together mayonnaise and mustard. Gradually add vinegar, whisking until smooth. Add cooled potatoes, cabbage, carrots, celery, and green onions. Toss to coat. Cover and chill in the refrigerator for 2 to 24 hours before serving. Toss before serving. Sprinkle with chopped turkey bacon.

MAKES 8 SERVINGS

*Tip: If desired, substitute 4 cups purchased shredded cabbage with carrot (coleslaw mix) for the shredded cabbage and carrots.

Garlic Mashed Potatoes

PREP: 25 minutes
SLOW COOK: 6 hours (low) or 3 hours (high)

NUTRITION FACTS PER SERVING

Calories 104
Fat 1 g
Cholesterol 3 mg
Sodium 226 mg
Carbohydrates 21 g
Fiber 1 g
Protein 3 g

3   pounds russet potatoes, peeled and cut into 2-inch pieces
6   cloves garlic, halved
1   bay leaf
2   14.5-ounce cans reduced-sodium chicken broth
1   cup fat-free milk
1   tablespoon butter
½   teaspoon ground white pepper
¼   teaspoon salt
¼   cup snipped fresh chives
     Whole fresh chives (optional)

1. In a 3½- or 4-quart slow cooker combine potatoes, garlic, and bay leaf. Pour broth over all in cooker.

2. Cover and cook on low-heat setting for 6 to 8 hours or on high-heat setting for 3 to 4 hours.

3. Drain potatoes in a colander over a bowl to catch cooking liquid. Discard bay leaf. Return potatoes to slow cooker. Mash to desired consistency with a potato masher.

4. In a small saucepan heat milk and butter until steaming and butter is almost melted. Add milk mixture, white pepper, salt, and enough of the reserved cooking liquid to the potato mixture to reach desired consistency. Reserve any remaining cooking liquid.* Stir in snipped chives. If desired, garnish each serving with whole chives. **MAKES 12 SERVINGS**

*Tip: If desired, return garlic mashed potatoes to slow cooker; keep warm on low-heat or warm setting for up to 2 hours. If mixture has thickened, stir in some of the reserved cooking liquid to reach desired consistency.

Cheesy Vegetable Bake

PREP: 30 minutes
BAKE: 40 minutes
STAND: 5 minutes
OVEN: 350°F

NUTRITION FACTS PER SERVING

Calories 104
Fat 4 g
Cholesterol 13 mg
Sodium 163 mg
Carbohydrates 10 g
Fiber 2 g
Protein 7 g

Nonstick cooking spray
2 16-ounce packages frozen broccoli, cauliflower, and carrots, thawed, rinsed, and drained*
1 12-ounce can evaporated fat-free milk
¼ cup finely chopped onion
2 tablespoons all-purpose flour
2 cloves garlic, minced
¼ teaspoon ground black pepper
¾ cup shredded reduced-fat sharp cheddar cheese (3 ounces)
½ of a 8-ounce package reduced-fat cream cheese (Neufchâtel), cut up and softened
⅔ cup soft whole wheat bread crumbs (1 slice)
2 tablespoons snipped fresh parsley and/or snipped fresh basil (optional)

1. Preheat oven to 350°F. Coat a 2-quart square baking dish with cooking spray. Arrange thawed vegetables in the baking dish. Set aside.

2. In a medium saucepan whisk together evaporated milk, onion, flour, garlic, and pepper. Cook and stir over medium heat until thickened and bubbly. Remove from heat. Add cheddar cheese and cream cheese, whisking until melted and smooth.

3. Evenly pour cheese mixture over vegetables. Toss gently to coat vegetables with sauce. Sprinkle with bread crumbs. Lightly coat crumbs with additional cooking spray.

4. Bake for 40 to 45 minutes or until bubbly and crumbs are lightly browned. Let stand for 5 minutes before serving. If desired, sprinkle with parsley and/or basil.
MAKES 12 SERVINGS

***Tip:** Thaw vegetables overnight in the refrigerator or place vegetables in a large colander. Run cool water over vegetables. Let stand for 15 minutes to drain.

Crisp Cornmeal Scones

PREP: 15 minutes
BAKE: 12 minutes
OVEN: 425°F

NUTRITION FACTS
PER 1½-INCH SCONE

Calories 155
Fat 6 g
Cholesterol 16 mg
Sodium 165 mg
Carbohydrates 24 g
Fiber 1 g
Protein 3 g

2   cups all-purpose flour
1   cup yellow cornmeal
2   tablespoons granulated sugar
1½ teaspoons baking powder
½   teaspoon salt
½   cup cold butter, coarsely
      shredded* or cubed
1   cup buttermilk
      Buttermilk
      Coarse sugar

1. Preheat oven to 425°F. In a large bowl whisk together flour, cornmeal, sugar, baking powder, and salt.

2. Add shredded butter to flour mixture; toss to distribute. (Or cut cubed butter into flour mixture with pastry blender until it resembles coarse crumbs.) Make a well in center of flour mixture. Add the 1 cup buttermilk; stir with spoon until moistened. Do not overmix. (If dough appears dry, add 1 to 2 tablespoons additional buttermilk.)

3. Turn dough out onto a floured surface. Gently knead by lifting and folding dough, four or five times, giving a quarter turn after each knead. Pat or roll into an 8-inch square, about ¾ inch thick. Cut into 1½- to 2-inch squares. Place squares 1 inch apart on ungreased baking sheet. Brush with buttermilk; sprinkle with coarse sugar. Bake for 12 to 15 minutes or until lightly browned; cool scones on a rack. Serve warm.
MAKES 16 TO 25 SCONES

*Tip: To shred butter, freeze the butter for 15 minutes. Using a grater, coarsely shred the cold butter. Toss into flour mixture or chill, loosely covered, until needed.

CHAPTER 11

Desserts

Raspberry Strudel Croissants

PREP: 20 minutes
BAKE: 12 minutes
OVEN: 375°F

NUTRITION FACTS PER STRUDEL

Calories 35
Fat 0 g
Cholesterol 0 mg
Sodium 30 mg
Carbohydrates 8 g
Fiber 0 g
Protein 1 g

¼   cup frozen red raspberries, thawed and drained, or fresh red raspberries
2   tablespoons low-sugar red raspberry preserves
¼   teaspoon finely shredded lemon peel
4   sheets frozen phyllo dough (14×9-inch rectangles), thawed
    Butter-flavor nonstick cooking spray
    Powdered sugar and/or finely shredded lemon peel (optional)
    Fresh raspberries (optional)

1. In a small bowl combine the ¼ cup raspberries, preserves, and the ¼ teaspoon lemon peel. Using a potato masher or the back of a large spoon, mash berry mixture.

2. Preheat oven to 375°F. Line a baking sheet with parchment paper; set aside. Unfold phyllo dough; place one sheet of the dough on a clean flat surface. (As you work, cover the remaining phyllo dough with plastic wrap to prevent it from drying out.) Lightly coat phyllo sheet with cooking spray. Place another sheet of the phyllo dough on top of the first sheet; coat with cooking spray. Repeat layering with two more sheets, coating each with cooking spray, for a stack of four sheets. Using a pastry wheel or pizza cutter, cut an 8½-inch circle in the dough (discard dough that is cut away to form the circle).

3. Cut circle into six wedges. Spread the raspberry filling over wedges, leaving a ¼-inch border around the raspberry layer. Starting at the wide end of each wedge, loosely roll toward the point. Place rolls, point sides down, 2 to 3 inches apart on the prepared baking sheet. Lightly coat filled croissants with cooking spray.

4. Bake for 12 to 14 minutes or until pastry is golden brown. Transfer to a wire rack; let cool. If desired, sprinkle croissants with powdered sugar and/or additional lemon peel. If desired, garnish with additional fresh raspberries.
MAKES 6 STRUDELS

Lemon Crepes

START TO FINISH: 25 minutes

NUTRITION FACTS
PER 1 CREPE + ¼ CUP
BERRY TOPPING

Calories 139
Fat 7 g
Cholesterol 33 mg
Sodium 22 mg
Carbohydrates 17 g
Fiber 1 g
Protein 4 g

2½ cups blueberries, raspberries, and/or sliced strawberries
2   to 3 teaspoons honey
¾   cup fat-free milk
½   cup all-purpose flour
1   egg
1   tablespoon canola oil
2   teaspoons sugar
1   teaspoon finely shredded lemon peel
½   cup mascarpone cheese, softened
2   tablespoons honey
    Finely shredded lemon peel (optional)

1. For berry topping, in a medium bowl combine berries and 2 to 3 teaspoons honey; toss gently to combine. Set aside.

2. For crepe batter, in a medium bowl combine milk, flour, egg, oil, sugar, and the 1 teaspoon lemon peel; whisk until smooth.

3. Heat a lightly greased medium skillet over medium-high heat; remove from heat. Spoon in 2 tablespoons of the batter; lift and tilt skillet to spread batter evenly. Return to heat; cook for 1 to 2 minutes or until brown on one side only. Invert skillet over paper towels; remove crepe. Repeat with the remaining batter, greasing skillet occasionally. If crepes are browning too quickly, reduce heat to medium.

4. In a small bowl stir together mascarpone cheese and 2 tablespoons honey. Spread the unbrowned side of each crepe with 1 tablespoon of the cheese mixture; fold crepe into quarters. Serve crepes with berry topping. If desired, garnish with additional lemon peel. **MAKES 10 SERVINGS**

Pistachio-Apple Baklava

PREP: 30 minutes   BAKE: 40 minutes   OVEN: 325°F

NUTRITION FACTS PER SERVING

Calories 88   *Fat* 3 g   *Cholesterol* 0 mg   *Sodium* 85 mg   *Carbohydrates* 14 g   *Fiber* 1 g   *Protein* 2 g

2   large cooking apples, cored and finely chopped (2 cups)

½   teaspoon finely shredded lemon peel

1   tablespoon lemon juice

1   tablespoon honey

¼   teaspoon ground allspice

¾   cup lightly salted pistachio nuts, toasted pecans (see tip, page 178), or toasted hazelnuts,* finely chopped

½   cup snipped dried cranberries
     Butter-flavor nonstick cooking spray

½   of a 16-ounce package frozen phyllo dough, thawed (twenty 9×14-inch sheets)

1. Preheat oven to 325°F. For apple filling, in a large bowl combine apples, lemon peel, lemon juice, honey, and allspice. Stir in pistachio nuts and cranberries. Set aside.

2. Coat a 2-quart square baking dish with cooking spray. Unroll phyllo dough. With kitchen shears or a long knife, cut the whole stack of phyllo in half crosswise to make forty 7×9-inch sheets. Keep phyllo covered with plastic wrap, removing sheets as needed.

3. Using 1 sheet of the phyllo dough at a time, layer 10 phyllo sheets in the dish, coating the top of each sheet with cooking spray and folding over any extra. Turn every other sheet a quarter turn to make even layers. Spread about 1 cup of the apple filling over phyllo in dish. Repeat layers twice. Layer remaining 10 phyllo dough sheets over apple filling, coating the top of each sheet with cooking spray.

4. Using a sharp knife, cut through phyllo and apple filling to make 9 squares; cut each square in half diagonally to make triangles. (Do not remove the pieces from dish.) Bake for 40 to 45 minutes or until golden brown. Cool completely on a wire rack. **MAKES 18 SERVINGS**

*Tip: To toast hazelnuts, preheat oven to 350°F. Spread nuts in a single layer in a shallow baking pan. Bake for 8 to 10 minutes or until lightly toasted, stirring once to toast evenly. Cool nuts slightly. Place the warm nuts on a clean kitchen towel; rub with the towel to remove the loose skins.

Pear-Cranberry Deep-Dish Pie

PREP: 40 minutes
BAKE: 55 minutes
COOL: 30 minutes
OVEN: 375°F

NUTRITION FACTS PER SERVING

Calories 169
Fat 4 g
Cholesterol 0 mg
Sodium 96 mg
Carbohydrates 34 g
Fiber 4 g
Protein 2 g

⅓   cup sugar
2   tablespoons all-purpose flour
¼   teaspoon ground nutmeg
¼   teaspoon ground ginger
6   pears, cored and sliced
     (2 to 2½ pounds total)
1   cup fresh or thawed frozen
     cranberries
1   recipe Pastry
1   tablespoon fat-free milk

1. Preheat oven to 375°F. For fruit filling, in an extra-large bowl combine sugar, flour, nutmeg, and ginger. Add pear slices and cranberries; toss gently to coat. Transfer to a 2-quart round baking dish or casserole.

2. On a lightly floured surface flatten Pastry dough. Using a rolling pin, roll dough from center to edge into a circle about 1 inch wider than the top of the baking dish or casserole. Using cookie cutters, cut a few small shapes from center of the pastry. Set shapes aside. Transfer the dough circle to the top of the fruit filling. Trim edge to fit the baking dish or casserole; if desired, crimp edge. Brush top of pastry and dough cutouts with milk. Place dough cutouts on pastry, leaving openings for air to vent.

3. Place baking dish or casserole on a foil-lined baking sheet. Bake for 55 to 60 minutes or until filling is very bubbly. Cool pie about 30 minutes on a wire rack. Serve warm or cool completely.
MAKES 10 SERVINGS

Pastry: In a medium bowl stir together ¾ cup cake flour, ¼ cup whole wheat flour, and ¼ teaspoon salt. Using a pastry blender, cut in ¼ cup chilled 60% to 70% tub-style vegetable oil spread until pieces are pea size. Sprinkle 1 tablespoon cold water over part of the flour mixture; gently toss with a fork. Push moistened dough to the side of the bowl. Repeat moistening flour mixture, using 1 tablespoon cold water at a time, until all is moistened (3 to 4 tablespoons total). Shape dough into a ball.

Fruit Tarts

START TO FINISH: 20 minutes

NUTRITION FACTS
PER TART

Calories 207
Fat 9 g
Cholesterol 14 mg
Sodium 189 mg
Carbohydrates 27 g
Fiber 2 g
Protein 3 g

1   cup fresh strawberries
½   of an 8-ounce package
    reduced-fat cream cheese
    (Neufchâtel), softened
1   tablespoon honey
1   4-ounce package (6)
    purchased graham cracker
    crumb tart shells
1½ cups assorted fresh berries
    or other chopped fruit
    (blueberries, kiwifruit,
    strawberries, and/or
    raspberries)

1. For cream cheese filling, mash
or puree the 1 cup strawberries
until saucy. In a medium bowl
stir cream cheese until smooth;
gradually blend in mashed berries.
Stir in honey. Divide filling among
six tart shells. Top with fresh fruit.
MAKES 6 TARTS

Make-Ahead Directions:
Prepare the cream cheese filling.
Cover and chill in the refrigerator
for up to 4 hours.

Caramel-Pear Bread Pudding

PREP: 25 minutes
BAKE: 50 minutes
STAND: 30 minutes
OVEN: 350°F

NUTRITION FACTS PER SERVING

Calories 147   *Fat* 2 g   *Cholesterol* 2 mg   *Sodium* 169 mg   *Carbohydrates* 28 g   *Fiber* 2 g   *Protein* 5 g

Nonstick cooking spray
8   slices whole grain white bread or whole grain wheat bread, cut into ½-inch pieces and dried* (about 5 cups dried bread cubes)
2   tablespoons tub-style vegetable oil spread, melted
2   red-skin pears
¼   cup dried cranberries (optional)
2   cups fat-free milk
¾   cup refrigerated or frozen egg product, thawed, or 3 eggs, lightly beaten
⅔   cup sugar-free caramel ice cream topping
½   teaspoon ground cinnamon
½   cup coarsely chopped pecans, toasted (optional)

1. Preheat oven to 350°F. Lightly coat a 2-quart rectangular or square baking dish with cooking spray; set aside. In a large bowl toss together dried bread and melted vegetable oil spread until coated. Core and chop one of the pears and add to the bread mixture along with the cranberries, if using. Gently toss to combine. Transfer to prepared baking dish.

2. In a medium bowl whisk together milk, eggs, ⅓ cup of the caramel topping, and the cinnamon. Slowly pour milk mixture evenly over bread mixture in baking dish. Using the back of a large spoon, gently press down bread mixture.

3. Bake, uncovered, for 50 to 60 minutes or until a knife inserted near center comes out clean. Let stand on a wire rack for 30 minutes.

4. To serve, cut pudding into 12 portions and place on serving plates. Quarter and core the remaining pear. Cut into very thin slices and place a few slices on each portion of pudding. If desired, sprinkle with pecans. Drizzle each serving with some of the remaining ⅓ cup caramel topping. Serve pudding warm.
MAKES 12 SERVINGS

*Tip: To dry bread cubes, preheat oven to 300°F. Place bread cubes in an ungreased 15×10×1-inch baking pan. Bake for 10 to 12 minutes or until bread cubes are dry and crisp, stirring once or twice.

Cherry-Chocolate Bread Pudding

PREP: 15 minutes
BAKE: 15 minutes
OVEN: 350°F

NUTRITION FACTS
PER SERVING

Calories 147
Fat 4 g
Cholesterol 1 mg
Sodium 152 mg
Carbohydrates 25 g
Fiber 3 g
Protein 7 g

Nonstick cooking spray
2   cups firm-textured whole-
    grain bread cubes (about
    3 ounces)
3   tablespoons snipped dried
    tart red cherries
1   tablespoon toasted wheat
    germ
⅔   cup fat-free milk
¼   cup semisweet chocolate
    pieces
⅓   cup refrigerated or frozen egg
    product, thawed
1   teaspoon finely shredded
    orange peel
½   teaspoon vanilla
    Frozen light whipped dessert
    topping, thawed (optional)
    Unsweetened cocoa powder
    (optional)

1. Preheat the oven to 350°F. Coat four 6-ounce individual soufflé dishes or custard cups with cooking spray. Divide bread cubes, cherries, and wheat germ among the dishes.

2. In a small saucepan combine milk and chocolate. Cook and stir over low heat until the chocolate is melted; remove from heat. If necessary, beat with a wire whisk until smooth.

3. In a small bowl gradually stir chocolate mixture into egg product. Stir in orange peel and vanilla. Pour mixture over bread cubes in the dishes. Press lightly with back of spoon to moisten bread.

4. Bake for 15 to 20 minutes or until the tops appear firm and a knife inserted near the centers comes out clean.

5. Serve warm. If desired, serve with whipped topping and sprinkle with cocoa powder. MAKES 4 SERVINGS

Make-Ahead Directions:
Prepare as directed through Step 3. Cover and chill up to 2 hours. Preheat oven to 350°F. Continue as directed in Step 4 and Step 5.

Key Lime Mousse

START TO FINISH: 15 minutes

NUTRITION FACTS PER SERVING

Calories 161
Fat 7 g
Cholesterol 14 mg
Sodium 121 mg
Carbohydrates 18 g
Fiber 1 g
Protein 6 g

1   12.3-ounce package silken-style extra-firm light tofu (fresh bean curd), cut up
½   of an 8-ounce package reduced-fat cream cheese (Neufchâtel), cut into cubes and softened
3   tablespoons honey
1   teaspoon finely shredded Key lime or Persian lime peel
1   tablespoon Key lime or Persian lime juice
1½ cups frozen light whipped dessert topping, thawed (about half of an 8-ounce container)
1½ cups fresh fruit (such as cut-up kiwifruit, strawberries, blueberries, raspberries, and/or cut-up mango)
    Honey (optional)

1. For mousse, in a medium mixing bowl combine tofu, cream cheese, 3 tablespoons honey, lime peel, and lime juice. Beat with an electric mixer on medium speed until smooth. Gently fold in whipped dessert topping until combined.

2. Place mousse in a bowl and top with fresh fruit or layer mousse and fruit in parfait glasses. If desired, drizzle with additional honey. **MAKES 6 SERVINGS**

Chocolate-Coconut Pudding

START TO FINISH: 30 minutes

NUTRITION FACTS PER SERVING

Calories 150   *Fat* 8 g   *Cholesterol* 0 mg   *Sodium* 111 mg   *Carbohydrates* 21 g   *Fiber* 2 g   *Protein* 2 g

1   cup unsweetened light coconut milk
¼   cup unsweetened cocoa powder
2   tablespoons cornstarch
¼   teaspoon salt
1¼ cups unsweetened almond milk
¼   cup packed brown sugar
2   tablespoons granulated sugar
4   ounces semisweet chocolate, chopped
½   teaspoon coconut extract
2   tablespoons unsweetened shredded coconut, toasted (see tip, page 135)

1. In a medium bowl whisk together coconut milk, cocoa powder, cornstarch, and salt. Set aside.

2. In a medium saucepan combine almond milk, brown sugar, and granulated sugar. Cook and stir over medium heat just until boiling. Add coconut milk mixture. Cook and stir just until mixture returns to boiling. Immediately reduce heat to low; cook and stir for 2 minutes more. Remove from heat. Add chocolate; let stand for 30 seconds. Add coconut extract; stir until smooth.

3. Spoon ¼ cup of the pudding into each of eight small dessert dishes, mugs, or pots de crème cups. Sprinkle with toasted coconut. Serve warm or chilled.
MAKES 8 SERVINGS

Blackberry-Banana Lemon Trifles

START TO FINISH: 10 minutes

NUTRITION FACTS
PER SERVING

Calories 165
Fat 3 g
Cholesterol 0 mg
Sodium 236 mg
Carbohydrates 35 g
Fiber 3 g
Protein 2 g

2   3.75-ounce containers lemon
    or vanilla sugar free-reduced-
    calorie ready-to-eat pudding*
1   banana, sliced
½   cup fresh blackberries,
    blueberries, raspberries, or
    sliced strawberries
1   100-calorie pack shortbread
    cookies, coarsely broken

1. Evenly divide one container of
pudding between two 8-ounce
straight-sided glasses. Top pudding
in glasses with half the banana
slices, half the blackberries, and half
the cookies. Repeat layers with the
remaining pudding, banana, berries,
and cookies. **MAKES 2 SERVINGS**

*Tip: If using vanilla pudding,
stir ¼ teaspoon finely shredded
lemon peel into each container of
pudding.

Rocky Road Parfaits

PREP: 15 minutes
STAND: 5 minutes

NUTRITION FACTS
PER PARFAIT

Calories 162
Fat 6 g
Cholesterol 2 mg
Sodium 386 mg
Carbohydrates 21 g
Fiber 1 g
Protein 7 g

1   4-serving-size package
    fat-free, sugar-free, reduced-
    calorie chocolate or chocolate
    fudge instant pudding mix
2   cups fat-free milk
½   cup frozen light whipped
    dessert topping, thawed
¼   cup unsalted peanuts,
    coarsely chopped
¼   cup tiny marshmallows
    Chocolate curls (optional)

1. Prepare pudding mix according
to package directions, using the
fat-free milk. Remove ¾ cup of
the pudding and place in a small
bowl; fold in whipped topping until
combined.

2. Divide remaining plain chocolate
pudding among four 6-ounce
glasses or dessert dishes. Top with
dessert topping mixture. Let stand
for 5 to 10 minutes or until set.

3. Sprinkle with peanuts and
marshmallows just before serving.
If desired, garnish with chocolate
curls. **MAKES 4 PARFAITS**

Make-Ahead Directions:
Prepare as directed through Step 2.
Cover and chill parfaits for up
to 24 hours. Serve as directed in
Step 3.

Chocolate-Raspberry Grillers

START TO FINISH: 18 minutes

NUTRITION FACTS PER SERVING

Calories 217   *Fat* 8 g   *Cholesterol* 10 mg   *Sodium* 180 mg   *Carbohydrates* 34 g   *Fiber* 3 g   *Protein* 4 g

8   ½-inch-thick slices challah or Hawaiian sweet bread
2   tablespoons butter, melted
4   to 6 ounces semisweet chocolate, finely chopped
1   cup raspberries
1   recipe Warm Chocolate Gravy

1. Heat a large heavy nonstick skillet over medium-low heat. Meanwhile, brush one side of each bread slice with some of the melted butter. Place half the bread slices, buttered sides down, on a plate. Sprinkle with chocolate and raspberries to within ¼ inch of crusts. Top with remaining bread, buttered sides up.

2. Place two sandwiches in the skillet. Weight with a heavy skillet. Cook over medium-low heat for 6 to 8 minutes or until chocolate is melted and bread is golden brown, turning once. Repeat with remaining sandwiches.

3. Slice in half to serve. Pass warm Chocolate Gravy for dipping.
MAKES 8 SERVINGS

Warm Chocolate Gravy: In a small bowl stir together ¼ cup sugar, 2 tablespoons unsweetened cocoa powder, and 1 tablespoon all-purpose flour; set aside. In a medium saucepan melt 1 tablespoon butter. Stir sugar mixture into melted butter until smooth. Gradually add 1¼ cups milk, stirring constantly. Cook and stir over medium heat until thickened and bubbly; cook and stir for 1 minute more. Makes 1¼ cups.

Coconut Fruit S'mores

START TO FINISH: 25 minutes

NUTRITION FACTS
PER S'MORE

Calories 150
Fat 9 g
Cholesterol 8 mg
Sodium 120 mg
Carbohydrates 25 g
Fiber 2 g
Protein 2 g

4   ounces dark or semisweet
    chocolate, chopped
    Nonstick cooking spray
3   tablespoons butter, melted
    and cooled
⅓   cup flaked coconut
12 marshmallows
1⅓ cups fresh blackberries
24 graham cracker squares

1. Preheat broiler. Place chocolate in a small microwave-safe bowl. Microwave on 50 percent power (medium) for 1½ minutes. Let stand for 5 minutes. Stir until smooth. Let cool for 10 minutes.

2. Line a baking sheet with foil; lightly coat with cooking spray.

3. Place melted butter in a shallow bowl; place coconut in another shallow bowl. Roll marshmallows in butter, then coconut. Thread berries and marshmallows on 6-inch skewers; place on prepared baking sheet. Sprinkle any remaining coconut on marshmallows. Spoon chocolate onto half the graham crackers and arrange on a platter.

4. Broil fruit kabobs 3 to 4 inches from heat for 1 to 1½ minutes or until coconut is lightly browned and marshmallows are puffed, turning once.

5. Immediately top each chocolate-coated graham cracker with a kabob. Use remaining graham cracker to pull marshmallows and berries off skewers to form sandwiches. **MAKES 12 S'MORES**

Grown-Up S'mores

START TO FINISH: 15 minutes

NUTRITION FACTS
PER S'MORE

Calories 145
Fat 3 g
Cholesterol 0 mg
Sodium 77 mg
Carbohydrates 29 g
Fiber 1 g
Protein 2 g

12 graham cracker squares
    (6 rectangles)
¼ cup raspberry or strawberry
    preserves
1 ounce bar dark chocolate,
    divided into 6 portions
1 teaspoon finely shredded
    orange peel
1 teaspoon snipped fresh
    rosemary
    Nonstick cooking spray
6 large marshmallows

1. Place six of the graham crackers in a single layer on a platter. Spread with raspberry preserves. Top each with a portion of chocolate; set aside. In a small bowl combine orange peel and rosemary; set aside. Lightly coat a long metal skewer with cooking spray. Thread marshmallows on the skewer, leaving ½ inch between marshmallows.

2. For a charcoal or gas grill, hold marshmallow kabob just above grill rack directly over medium heat about 2 minutes or until marshmallows are soft and lightly toasted, turning occasionally.

3. Working quickly, use a fork to push one marshmallow onto each chocolate-topped graham cracker. Sprinkle with orange peel mixture. Top with remaining graham cracker squares. **MAKES 6 S'MORES**

Loaded Oatmeal Cookies

PREP: 30 minutes
BAKE: 9 minutes per batch
OVEN: 350°F

NUTRITION FACTS PER COOKIE

Calories 79   *Fat* 4 g   *Cholesterol* 11 mg   *Sodium* 45 mg   *Carbohydrates* 12 g   *Fiber* 1 g   *Protein* 2 g

¼   cup butter, softened
½   cup packed brown sugar
⅓   cup granulated sugar
1   teaspoon ground cinnamon
½   teaspoon baking soda
⅛   teaspoon salt
1   egg
1   teaspoon vanilla
¾   cup all-purpose flour
¾   cup rolled oats
¼   cup flaxseed meal
¼   cup wheat germ
2   ounces dark chocolate, finely chopped
¼   cup dried cranberries
¼   cup chopped walnuts, toasted (see tip, page 178)

1. Preheat oven to 350°F. In a large mixing bowl beat butter with an electric mixer on medium to high speed for 30 seconds. Add brown sugar, granulated sugar, cinnamon, baking soda, and salt. Beat until combined, scraping sides of bowl occasionally. Beat in egg and vanilla until combined. Beat in flour. Stir in rolled oats, flaxseed meal, wheat germ, chocolate, cranberries, and walnuts (dough will be a little crumbly).

2. Drop dough by rounded teaspoons 2 inches apart onto an ungreased cookie sheets. Bake for 9 to 11 minutes or until tops are lightly browned. Let cookies cool on cookie sheet for 1 minute. Transfer cookies to wire rack to cool completely.

MAKES ABOUT 30 COOKIES

Must-Have Chocolate Chip Cookies

PREP: 20 minutes
BAKE: 10 minutes per batch
OVEN: 350°F

NUTRITION FACTS PER COOKIE

Calories 87
Fat 4 g
Cholesterol 3 mg
Sodium 47 mg
Carbohydrates 12 g
Fiber 1 g
Protein 2 g

1	cup raisins
½	cup boiling water
½	cup peanut butter
¼	cup butter, softened
½	cup sugar
½	cup refrigerated or frozen egg product, thawed
1	teaspoon ground cinnamon
1	teaspoon vanilla
½	teaspoon baking soda
½	cup all-purpose flour
1¼	cups regular rolled oats
1	cup semisweet chocolate pieces or chunks

1. Preheat oven to 350°F. In a small bowl combine raisins and boiling water; set aside.

2. In a large mixing bowl combine peanut butter and butter; beat with an electric mixer on medium speed for 30 seconds. Add sugar, egg product, cinnamon, vanilla, and baking soda. Beat until combined. Add the flour; beat until smooth. Stir in the oats.

3. Drain the raisins; stir raisins and chocolate pieces into oat mixture.

4. Drop dough by rounded teaspoons onto ungreased cookie sheets. Bake about 10 minutes or until lightly browned. Transfer to wire racks; let cool.
MAKES 40 COOKIES

Triple-Chocolate-Mint Sandwich Cookies

PREP: 20 minutes
CHILL: 1 hour
BAKE: 6 minutes per batch
OVEN: 350°F

NUTRITION FACTS PER
2 SANDWICH COOKIES

Calories 141
Fat 5 g
Cholesterol 1 mg
Sodium 63 mg
Carbohydrates 22 g
Fiber 1 g
Protein 2 g

½ cup granulated sugar
3   tablespoons canola oil
2   ounces white baking
    chocolate, melted
2   egg whites
¾   teaspoon mint flavoring
½   teaspoon butter flavoring
1⅓ cups all-purpose flour
½   teaspoon baking powder
¼   teaspoon salt
1   tablespoon unsweetened
    cocoa powder
½   cup powdered sugar
2   ounces bittersweet chocolate,
    melted
1   to 2 tablespoons water
1   ounce white baking chocolate,
    melted (optional)
    Very small fresh mint leaves
    (optional)

1. In a medium bowl combine granulated sugar, oil, 2 ounces melted white chocolate, egg whites, mint flavoring, and butter flavoring; stir until well mixed. In a small bowl stir together flour, baking powder, and salt. Add the flour mixture to the egg white mixture; stir just until combined. Cover and chill dough for 1 to 24 hours or until firm enough to roll into balls.

2. Preheat oven to 350°F. Place cocoa powder in a small bowl. Shape dough into ¾-inch balls (1 teaspoon dough each). Roll balls in cocoa powder to coat. Place balls 1½ inches apart on ungreased cookie sheets. Flatten balls with the bottom of a glass to about 1¼-inch-diameter circles.

3. Bake for 6 to 7 minutes or just until edges are firm. Transfer to a wire rack; cool.

4. For chocolate filling, in a small bowl whisk together powdered sugar, melted bittersweet chocolate, and enough of the 1 to 2 tablespoons water to make a smooth spreadable filling. (If mixture seems too thin, allow it to stand a few minutes before using.)

5. Spread the bottoms of half the cookies with chocolate filling, using about 1 teaspoon filling on each. Top with remaining cookies, bottom sides down, to make sandwich cookies.

6. If desired, place the 1 ounce melted white chocolate in a small resealable plastic bag. Seal bag. Using scissors, snip off a very small corner from bag. Drizzle white chocolate over tops of cookies; place mint leaves on top.
MAKES 16 SANDWICH COOKIES

Tip: To store, layer undrizzled sandwich cookies between sheets of waxed paper in an airtight container; cover. Store at room temperature for up to 3 days or freeze for up to 3 months. To serve, thaw cookies if frozen. If desired, drizzle with white chocolate as directed in Step 6.

Pumpkin Blondies

PREP: 10 minutes
BAKE: 20 minutes
OVEN: 350°F

NUTRITION FACTS PER BAR

Calories 137
Fat 6 g
Cholesterol 13 mg
Sodium 104 mg
Carbohydrates 19 g
Fiber 1 g
Protein 2 g

Nonstick cooking spray
1   cup white whole wheat flour
½   cup unbleached all-purpose flour
1   tablespoon flaxseed meal
1½ teaspoons baking powder
½   teaspoon salt
½   teaspoon ground cinnamon
¼   teaspoon baking soda
¼   teaspoon ground nutmeg
⅛   teaspoon ground allspice
⅓   cup canola oil
3   tablespoons butter, melted
1   tablespoon molasses
1⅓ cups packed dark brown sugar
½   cup canned pumpkin
1   egg
1   egg white
1   teaspoon vanilla
½   cup coarsely chopped walnuts

1. Preheat oven to 350°F. Coat a 13×9×2-inch baking pan with cooking spray or line with parchment paper; set aside. In a medium bowl combine whole wheat flour, all-purpose flour, flaxseed meal, baking powder, salt, cinnamon, baking soda, nutmeg, and allspice; set aside.

2. In a large mixing bowl beat oil, butter, and molasses with an electric mixer on medium speed until combined. Add brown sugar and beat until smooth. Add pumpkin, beating until combined. Beat in egg, egg white, and vanilla until combined. Add to sugar mixture, beating just until flour mixture is moistened.

3. Spread batter into prepared pan. Sprinkle with walnuts. Bake for 20 to 22 minutes or until a wooden toothpick inserted near center comes out clean. Cool completely in pan on a wire rack. Cut into bars.
MAKES 24 BARS

Index &
Metric

How Recipes Are Analyzed

The Better Homes and Gardens® Test Kitchen uses nutrition-analysis software to determine the nutritional value of a single serving of a recipe. Here are some factors to keep in mind regarding each analysis:

- Analyses do not include optional ingredients.
- The first serving size listed is analyzed when a range is given. For example, if a recipe makes 4 to 6 servings, the Nutrition Facts are based on 4 servings.
- When ingredient choices (such as butter or margarine) appear in a recipe, the first one mentioned is used for analysis.
- When milk is a recipe ingredient, the analysis has been calculated using fat-free (skim) milk unless otherwise noted.

Metric Information

The charts on this page provide a guide for converting measurements from the U.S. customary system, which is used throughout this book, to the metric system.

Product Differences

Most of the ingredients called for in the recipes in this book are available in most countries. However, some are known by different names. Here are some common American ingredients and their possible counterparts:

- Sugar (white) is granulated, fine granulated, or castor sugar.
- Powdered sugar is icing sugar.
- All-purpose flour is enriched bleached, or unbleached white household flour. When self-rising flour is used in place of all-purpose flour in a recipe that calls for leavening, omit the leavening agent (baking soda or baking powder) and salt.
- Light-color corn syrup is golden syrup.
- Cornstarch is cornflour.
- Baking soda is bicarbonate of soda.
- Vanilla or vanilla extract is vanilla essence.
- Green, red, or yellow sweet peppers are capsicums or bell peppers.
- Golden raisins are sultanas.

Volume and Weight

The United States traditionally uses cup measures for liquid and solid ingredients. The chart below shows the approximate imperial and metric equivalents. If you are accustomed to weighing solid ingredients, the following approximate equivalents will be helpful.

- 1 cup butter, castor sugar, or rice = 8 ounces = ½ pound = 250 grams
- 1 cup flour = 4 ounces = ¼ pound = 125 grams
- 1 cup icing sugar = 5 ounces = 150 grams

Canadian and U.S. volume for a cup measure is 8 fluid ounces (237 ml), but the standard metric equivalent is 250 ml.

1 British imperial cup is 10 fluid ounces.

In Australia, 1 tablespoon equals 20 ml, and there are 4 teaspoons in the Australian tablespoon.

Spoon measures are used for smaller amounts of ingredients. Although the size of the tablespoon varies slightly in different countries, for practical purposes and for recipes in this book, a straight substitution is all that's necessary. Measurements made using cups or spoons always should be level unless stated otherwise.

Common Weight Range Replacements

IMPERIAL / U.S.	METRIC
½ ounce	15 g
1 ounce	25 g or 30 g
4 ounces (¼ pound)	115 g or 125 g
8 ounces (½ pound)	225 g or 250 g
16 ounces (1 pound)	450 g or 500 g
1¼ pounds	625 g
1½ pounds	750 g
2 pounds or 2¼ pounds	1,000 g or 1 Kg

Oven Temperature Equivalents

FAHRENHEIT SETTING	CELSIUS SETTING*	GAS SETTING
300°F	150°C	Gas Mark 2 (very low)
325°F	160°C	Gas Mark 3 (low)
350°F	180°C	Gas Mark 4 (moderate)
375°F	190°C	Gas Mark 5 (moderate)
400°F	200°C	Gas Mark 6 (hot)
425°F	220°C	Gas Mark 7 (hot)
450°F	230°C	Gas Mark 8 (very hot)
475°F	240°C	Gas Mark 9 (very hot)
500°F	260°C	Gas Mark 10 (extremely hot)
Broil	Broil	Grill

*Electric and gas ovens may be calibrated using celsius. However, for an electric oven, increase celsius setting 10 to 20 degrees when cooking above 160°C. For convection or forced air ovens (gas or electric), lower the temperature setting 25°F/10°C when cooking at all heat levels.

Baking Pan Sizes

IMPERIAL / U.S.	METRIC
9×1½-inch round cake pan	22- or 23×4-cm (1.5 L)
9×1½-inch pie plate	22- or 23×4-cm (1 L)
8×8×2-inch square cake pan	20×5-cm (2 L)
9×9×2-inch square cake pan	22- or 23×4.5-cm (2.5 L)
11×7×1½-inch baking pan	28×17×4-cm (2 L)
2-quart rectangular baking pan	30×19×4.5-cm (3 L)
13×9×2-inch baking pan	34×22×4.5-cm (3.5 L)
15×10×1-inch jelly roll pan	40×25×2-cm
9×5×3-inch loaf pan	23×13×8-cm (2 L)
2-quart casserole	2 L

U.S. / Standard Metric Equivalents

⅛ teaspoon = 0.5 ml

¼ teaspoon = 1 ml

½ teaspoon = 2 ml

1 teaspoon = 5 ml

1 tablespoon = 15 ml

2 tablespoons = 25 ml

¼ cup = 2 fluid ounces = 50 ml

⅓ cup = 3 fluid ounces = 75 ml

½ cup = 4 fluid ounces = 125 ml

⅔ cup = 5 fluid ounces = 150 ml

¾ cup = 6 fluid ounces = 175 ml

1 cup = 8 fluid ounces = 250 ml

2 cups = 1 pint = 500 ml

1 quart = 1 litre